THE ADVENTURES OF
a Girl Wearing PEARLS

JAN CONSTABLE

ISBN: 978-1-4834-5156-5 (sc)
ISBN: 978-1-4834-5157-2 (e)

Because of the dynamic nature of the Internet, any web addresses or links contained in this book may have changed since publication and may no longer be valid. The views expressed in this work are solely those of the author and do not necessarily reflect the views of the publisher, and the publisher hereby disclaims any responsibility for them.

Any people depicted in stock imagery provided by Thinkstock are models, and such images are being used for illustrative purposes only.
Certain stock imagery © Thinkstock.

Lulu Publishing Services rev. date: 5/31/2016

ONCE THE SAND OF DUBAI HAS SETTLED ON YOUR

SHOULDERS, YOU NEVER SHAKE IT OFF.

ANONYMOUS

For my lovely Mike

Without whom this book would not have been possible.
His encouragement and support has been boundless

With all my love

Special thanks are due:

U3A Marbella and **Inland's Writing Your Memoir Class**,
where I received enormous support and encouragement
from Christine Kemzura and my fellow scribes.

Janet Rowles for her artwork

Melanie Chalk for her editing skills

My blog buddies, from far and wide, who continually supported me

My Dubai chums, both old and new, always by my side

Dubai, itself, without whom there would have been no tale to tell

Contents

An Invitation!

Hello. My name is Jan and I am inviting you to tag along with me, if you will, to enjoy the highs and lows of my exploits whilst I begin telling you about my experiences when I very unexpectedly found myself tiptoeing into the 'bloody abroad' without a by your leave or do you mind. This was my husband's fault as he worked for an international oil company, and where does oil come from? Yes, you have guessed it, the 'bloody abroad'; so off he went with me trotting behind, somewhat reluctantly.

Laugh and cry but, most of all, I implore you to be amazed and amused in equal measure and, perhaps, say 'Golly gosh, how times have changed,' and pose the question, 'Would I have been such a loyal camp follower to Dubai or would I have said no way José or, maybe at the last moment, would curiosity have got the better of me?' Who knows!

In 1970, in my early twenties, I was catapulted into Dubai in the Trucial Oman States from leafy Surrey by dint of being married to an oil executive. 'So what?' I can hear you say. Well in those distant days, hardly a soul on God's earth had heard of Dubai, unlike today when Dubai is never out of the news. It was and still is a little desert kingdom ruled by a sheikh, lapped by the Persian Gulf and is hideously hot during the summer. What a prospect; it sure didn't sound too much like a walk in the park to me. Hey ho.

Before we start on our journey together, tiptoeing into the unknown, I must explain I really wasn't too well equipped for this adventure. I thought my destiny lay somewhere in the Home Counties (of England) where I was brought up and that was, perhaps, where I would remain.

On reflection, how dull my life might have been as I sure would never have had these tales to tell — and would never have been able to write about 'The Adventures of a Girl Wearing Pearls'.

Bombshell!

I will never forget May 8th 1970 as it was the day my life, as I knew it, was to irrevocably change forever. Mike, my husband, had been posted to Dubai in the Trucial Oman States at a time when nobody had even heard of Dubai and the only information that could be gleaned from the Board of Trade was that it imported massive quantities of gold, had no official exports and was hideously hot during the summer. In those days, there was no option and wives were expected to accompany their husbands wherever they were posted, donning a stiff upper lip at all times or, more to the point, being seen and not heard. I think it was called towing the line!

It was with total fear and trepidation that we advanced towards the dreaded day, with so many plans and so much to do, not least of which was stocking up on essentials, as back then Dubai was not the shopping Mecca that it is today. I was briefed as to what was available and what I should definitely consider taking with me, and one considerable item was cosmetics. To that end I can vividly remember visiting Elizabeth Arden in Bond Street and attempting to order enough cosmetics to last a year; it sounds quite preposterous now. Oh, and J-cloths — why I thought we needed about 500 I will never know; and then there was the question of hosting company soirées which would require, as far as I could make out, buying up the whole of Mappin & Webb. What a nightmare!

For clothes, it was suggested that one should take a sufficient amount to cover every eventuality, but what was every eventuality, I wondered. My first priority was to be well-turned-out at all times, disregarding the sweltering temperatures; consequently, I embarked on a dizzy round of shopping and fittings for cocktail dresses, evening dresses and tea dresses, as well as all the other essentials, including tennis, golf and swimming gear. At this stage, I really had no idea at all as to whether my acquisitions would be appropriate or whether I would need to be covered from head to toe in a black abaya and burka, or indeed if I would ever see the light of day, this being an Arab country where women did not have too many rights.

The dreaded day was fast approaching, the packers had been, the house was let, the car was sold, our lovely dog Lucy was going to stay with my parents and numerous farewell parties had been attended. It was like sleepwalking into an abyss.

Our farewells had been made. 'When will we see you again?' chums chorused.

'Not sure,' was the reply, 'maybe sooner rather than later'.

May 8th had arrived and I was dressed to kill in one of my beautiful new outfits, in retrospect more appropriate for Ladies' Day at Ascot than for heading to the desert. We were driven to Heathrow by my parents and joined there by Mike's parents and chums, and this was when realization dawned — there was no going back. I managed to get through immigration but then it was a total collapse of 'stout party', the stout party being me. On reflection, I think I cried all the way to Dubai. Oh what misery, even my beautiful new clothes didn't lift the spirits or the wonderment of being on my first international flight, or the concern of the cabin crew. My poor Mike was wondering just what could be done to console me; I think I kept saying 'I want to go home' but we were helter-skeltering into the unknown, possibly both as terrified as each other.

Dubai Creek, May 1970

Imprisoned!

In my haze, I heard the captain announce, 'Please fasten your seatbelts; we are preparing to land'. Oh my God, Doomsville here I come. After a quick wash and brush-up, I was as ready as I was going to be to face my new world.

The doors were opened and we bade our farewells to a rather concerned cabin crew, who were onward bound for Bombay, and descended into the hellish warm night that Dubai offered. The only passenger building at Dubai Airport was akin to a Nissan hut, very basic indeed. Mike was greeted by Samir, a decidedly plump young Palestinian who had been detailed to meet and greet and take us to the hotel, which was minutes from the airport and reached via a slim road straddled by the desert.

The hotel was madly named the 'Riviera' — to my mind this was nothing like the Riviera I knew and loved in the South of France, but hey ho. The road ran alongside the Creek, which was littered with dhows, the Arab sailing boats, cows, goats and a few Arabs, being the sum total of any humanity that I could detect at that late hour. The entrance to the hotel was dark and very gloomy, with hardly a light in sight, and I was soon to discover that I was now in real Arab land. There was a dingy reception area and a very dingy bar that was well hidden behind a curtain; not a very encouraging start to my new world. And not a European in sight; was this Shell's idea of a joke?

We reached our room and to my dismay it too was dark and gloomy, but it did have a view of the Creek. Morning came round very quickly when Mike had to rise at 6am and be ready for the off at 6.30am, with no idea where he was being taken or when he might return. I found myself all alone in this hellhole, not knowing anyone, anything or what to do; it took me until about mid-morning to pluck up the courage to venture down to the reception area.

My recollection of the first few days was like living life in hell. It was far too hot to venture outside and, in any case, we were both under the impression that it was unacceptable for a Western woman to be out unescorted and, consequently, I was effectively a prisoner. We had to adapt, but how? Mike was settled into a vastly different work routine, leaving at 6.30am and arriving back at approximately 2.30pm. During these hours I had to amuse myself and, as luck would have it, I came across a British Overseas Airways Corporation (BOAC) crew in reception. What a delight; this was to be the turning point as I discovered that many of them lived near our house in Surrey so we had lots in common. Thank God, I now had a few playmates. Obviously, this was a far cry from life in Camberley where, in those days, no young married woman would have been seen being chatted-up by lots of men. Another learning curve, but my sanity was saved and consequently Mike could relax a little too.

Along came the day of our first dinner invitation, to the Shell General Manager's house and, of course, I wore one of my many little outfits! What a silly billy, their house was over the other side of the Creek on its own in the middle of the desert in a location called Jumeirah. What a Charlie I must have looked ready for a day in town but not for building sandcastles! And I was so very hot; I didn't fall into that trap ever, ever again.

Dinner was very formal, something I was going to have to get used to very quickly. The General Manager's wife presided at one end of the table and, to direct the servants, she rang a little silver bell at the sound of which they appeared in double-quick time. I was mesmerized but I soon acquired one of those little marvels; unfortunately, it was to be a while before 'my Ali' had any idea as to what he was supposed to do on hearing the 'tingalingling', and I wasn't too sure either! Actually, it was like playing a game of chance and it didn't take me long before I realized that Ali and I had no idea on God's earth what we were up to!

Things were looking up with one dinner party under our belts and we were brave enough to venture for a little walk outside the hotel along the Creek and over the sand patches, as not many buildings abounded the Creek back then. On one such evening we were hailed by a bunch of young British chaps who were obviously having a great time crowded onto a first floor balcony above. I think the building was the British Bank of the Middle East, which was in Al Nasar Square.

One of them was firing shots over the square in time to the music, which was the 1812 Overture, and a cacophony of sound ricocheted over the square. This was music to my ears and so unexpected; it sounded as if they were having a whale of a time. What a surprise, he wasn't very popular with his superiors and was shipped off to Saudi Arabia in double-quick time.

'Are you lost?' they yelled. 'Come and join us.' I was up the stairs like a shot with Mike following, slightly warily. We were scooped up by these young people, chaps from Gray Mackenzie which was the Persian Gulf's answer to the East India Company, as well as young bankers, engineers and accountants. They were all pioneers in their fashion, and by the time we departed I had my first tennis date and we also had our first curry lunch date — Pandora's box had finally been opened!

Dante's Inferno!

We had survived two weeks in a place akin to Dante's Inferno, which was not a bad effort, especially as this was due to our own ingenuity and those stiff upper lips. Actually mine quivered on many occasions but that's another story.

Mike had little time to be aware of his surroundings having been pushed into the deep end. The first plant of his Bitumen Supply Company was being commissioned and he was required to be in attendance almost 24/7; I, on the other hand, had all the time in the world to reflect and to wonder 'what if', but most of the time I was utterly bemused. I would look out of the window of the hotel gazing at all the activity along the Creek where the dhows were moored. The activity was non-stop with the ragtag crew members forever sluicing the decks, mending the sails or making ropes, and the most important member, 'Cookie', stirring the giant cooking pot containing yet another curry to sustain them.

These dhows were kept in pristine condition, so much so that most of them had Persian carpets strewn over the decks where the crew would sleep under the stars at night. These boats had little in the way of 'facilities' and the chaps used buckets of water hauled up from the Creek for their ablutions, and their toilet facilities were both fascinating and ingenious. At the stern of every ship was a wonderful arrangement affectionately called a 'thunder box'. This was a seat installed inside a little house where they would perform as if it was the most normal routine in the world. So there we have it, my room with a 'view'; a world away from my room with a 'view' in Surrey.

At this stage we had been living in the hotel for two weeks waiting for news of our permanent accommodation, and it came one day like a hammer blow. We were being allocated an apartment one block along from the hotel, which at that stage had not even been finished. I was devastated that we were not going to Jumeirah where the other expats lived in their exotic villas, at least that is what I thought, oh what ignominy. Nothing could be done about this as it was a decision from up high, oh dear. The Creek to me seemed like the Rubicon, and how was I ever going to cross to the other side where Jumeirah lay?

Now I had other things to tax my mind, such as furniture. Was there such a thing as a furniture shop in Dubai? Help was at hand, or so I thought. The GM's wife rang to make a date to take me shopping. The due day arrived and I was collected from the hotel by her driver and we set off over the subka tracks – there were few tarmac roads in Dubai in those days – and very quickly arrived at a single storey building on the edge of town. Although only about five minutes from the hotel, it was a very bumpy journey which took forever but, on arrival, wonder of wonders it turned out to be a furniture emporium. We alighted from the car and entered — oh my God, everything was covered in sand and dust, and the choice was negligible. There was one sofa set, an assortment of teak easy chairs, dining sets, and beds with frames made of wood on which mattresses rested. Slumberland it was not! I was then whisked to another such shop; this one was nestling behind some sand dune, address unknown, and Knightsbridge it certainly wasn't. Again, it contained a similar selection of furniture but this time, amazingly, it had a sofa set in blue and my spirits lifted as it was not as dour as the oatmeal one in the previous shop. I voiced this to the GM's wife who informed me in no uncertain words that I would not be allowed the blue set as the sofa had four seats.

'Why?' I asked.

'You are a junior wife and only allowed a three seater sofa.'

Boy, that put me in my place. To add further insult, I was informed that the driver would have to drop me halfway into town as she had a luncheon date at the Petroleum Wives' Club and time was short. So there I was, picking my way over the sand strewn paths back to the hotel wishing that I was far, far away and then a thought occurred to me. Was I not now a Petroleum Wife? Albeit one who was a little wet behind the ears!

I took refuge in the hotel which was fast becoming my 'home from home' away from home. What a shock all this was to the system; my life had really been turned upside down and obviously there was no going back to genteel Camberley, where my days had been happily filled with fripperies, lunch and tennis dates, hair appointments, flower arranging and cookery classes, as well as enjoying and arranging wonderful dinner parties and, not least, being invited to sumptuous Army balls. This part of the world being Army territory, in today's parlance I would have been the very epitome of a 'lady that lunches'. On reflection, although all this was to stand me in good stead, I should really have been spending my time developing a career as I had had an excellent education, but I was brought up to be a 'girl in pearls' and I didn't know anything else. No wonder I was finding my new situation a little tricky. It sure was going to take all the ingenuity that I could muster to make something of the very extraordinary situation I found myself in and not to run away!

Holy Moses!

Aren't humans strange — there I was in a totally alien environment but, on occasions, was able to raise a little smile and recognize the absurdity of the situation that I had been catapulted into.

A pattern had developed by dint of necessity. Mike was up and away very early in the morning after which I was left to my own devices. I would take a deep breath, count to ten, and then venture down to the restaurant for breakfast, where most tables seemed to be taken up with the BOAC crew.

Initially, I found this terrifying but had to brazen this out somehow; but how? I needed a prop for moral support and came up with what I thought was a splendid idea, and that was arming myself with a slightly old newspaper from which I could safely hide behind. I figured that this would give me some much needed Dutch courage and also, laughably, I might appear learned whilst attempting to do the crossword, the easy one of course! It has to be remembered that in those distant days it definitely was not a normal occurrence for a lone woman to be seen floating around a hotel in Dubai, especially at breakfast time!

I thought this ploy might just give me an excuse to ask for help with the clues, and would be a subtle way of 'chatting up the boys'! Without being armed with this prop I would have been far too terrified and possibly would have never set foot outside the room, but then I would have starved to death. There was no room service in those days!

This ploy worked and I soon knew everyone there was to know in the hotel, but more to the point they all knew me! On occasions, this seemed like the whole of BOAC, which I found quite extraordinary. Then there was Mohammed, the dashing hotel manager, and his boss, the wonderfully named Sheik Elias, who was the hotel owner, and who, incidentally, was from that exotic sounding country of Lebanon. You might have detected that there was not another woman in sight!

In retrospect, it never occurred to me that I must have appeared particularly stupid not knowing the answers to the most elementary of cryptic crossword questions. Oh my, they must have felt so sorry for Mike being married to such a nincompoop! But a resourceful one nevertheless!

We had been in Dubai for three weeks and were now the proud owners of an air-conditioned car, but initially it was tricky as just driving on the right was a challenge in itself without the added problem of negotiating the narrow creekside road, where we encountered all manner of obstacles.

These came in the form of various animals, such as goats, sheep and camels, and then there were the coolies pulling their giant carts alongside the dhows, plying for work to carry goods to the Souk. Oh my, what confusion; all I could say is that I hoped we were well insured! I was sure my driving techniques would have to dramatically change if I was ever going to master this latest challenge. Total confusion seemed to be the order of the day!

Wonderful, I thought, we can now go for a spin, but where to? It didn't take too long though, even for the dim-witted like me, to register that there was nowhere to go. This was sand dune country after all!

We also had our first glimpse of the apartment, which was to be our home for the foreseeable future. It was on the sixth floor of this new block, a stone's throw from the hotel. Outwardly, it was not very inspiring; it was very grey in appearance, and actually reminded me of an ancient old battleship that was surely built to last!

Our luck was in as the lift was working, so up we went. Well, the front door opened into an enormous vestibule that was big enough to hold a dance but was really quite dark. However, the other four rooms – the lounge, dining room and two bedrooms – all opened onto a large balcony, which overlooked the Creek. My goodness, we were going to have four rooms with a view, how amazing!

Thank goodness provision had been made for air-conditioning. But surprise, surprise, because the vestibule didn't figure in the furniture schedule allocated to us by Shell, which was based on Mike's grade, no furniture was to be provided for this vast space! Another obstacle to be overcome, but we were getting used to them!

The concerted opinion was that we would probably be in the hotel for at least another three weeks, due to reasons beyond our control. But that wasn't everything, with the most important issue being that the ship carrying our kit wasn't due to anchor until then, as well as the fact that the apartment was not quite finished. What to do?

At that very moment, some angels came to my rescue in the form of yet another BOAC crew together with two RAF chaps, who had a secret up their sleeves, which they were about to divulge. Holy Moses, there was a sailing club up the Creek situated on the far side of the Al Maktoum Bridge, and would I like to join them? Would I, this was music to my ears as I loved sailing, having been mucking about on boats since my early childhood; consequently, I was a real Swallows and Amazon girl.

I was invited to tag along. What a surprise, this place was nothing like a sailing club I had ever visited before. There were no refinements; all I could see were assorted tables outside a makeshift clubhouse and situated under a barasti awning, where a few hardy chaps were enjoying a beer. Oh my God it was as hot as Hades!

It transpired that the idea for the sailing club was the brainchild of some BOAC personnel to give them an outlet whilst on stopovers to Hong Kong and beyond. I was soon in my element. I was offered a sail and introduced to my fellow sailors, who were mostly military personnel from a base in Sharjah, which was up the road from Dubai. My knowledge of the area was so scant it could actually have been up the Khyber for all I knew!

I was becoming accustomed to being the only girl about the place, but this had certain advantages. I never had to rig my own boat as there was always help at hand, so there were some perks to be had. This unlikely little spot nestling under the Al Maktoum Bridge beside a very muddy creek, which was often prone to flooding, was to become my haven and sanity saver.

It was doubly welcome as all items on the Furnishing List had been located and ordered and the only other thing outstanding was finding a houseboy. I had quickly discovered that no self-respecting memsahib could hold her head high without one. Yes, I was on my way to being transformed into one myself!

To this end, Mohammed at the hotel had taken it upon himself to find a suitable candidate. His name was Ali and, wonder of wonders, he was the best houseboy in the world, a real paragon. There was nothing he would not do or could not do; it was quite obvious that he had to be hired on the spot. I'm not sure whether we would ever have actually called him a paragon, but that's another story!

Smoke Signal!

We were still playing the waiting game! It was over six weeks since we had arrived in Dubai and we were champing at the bit to move into the apartment. It was if we had been shunted into a siding with no knowledge of when the next train would arrive; it was like playing a game of chess but without knowing who was going to make the next move.

With Ali's elbow grease and my newly acquired status as 'Memsahib' directing operations, the apartment was as ready to receive its two VIP tenants as it would ever be, except for one vital fact — our kit from the UK was still on board the ship, which was somewhere offshore. So near and yet so far, and there was no news as to when it would be offloaded and delivered.

At long last we received a smoke signal to say the shipment had been offloaded and was at the quayside, waiting for coolies with their carts to be loaded up and trundled alongside the Creek to its final destination, our new home; what a thrill.

It took some time but eventually everything was delivered by this rag, tag and bobtail army of coolies, and I lost no time in unpacking. It was just like Christmas. It had been such a long time since I had last seen the contents of these boxes that I had forgotten what had been packed in the first place except, of course, for the 500 J-cloths! We were now ready to actually call Apartment 603, The Almulla Building, Creekside, Dubai our home for the foreseeable future. Fond farewells were made to one and all at the hotel and off we trotted. It seemed too good to be true as nothing was ever plain sailing and this little exercise was no exception, especially when you were trying to set-up home way out of your comfort zone and in temperatures that would literally have singed your eyebrows off!

We hadn't even been in the wretched place a day before we were about to experience our first crisis. It was discovered that none of the air-conditioners were working as they had not been charged with any cooling agent, namely Freon gas, without which they would not cool. Boy, it really felt as if we were experiencing the full wrath of Dante as outside the temperatures were well above 40°C and inside it was not much better, and far too hot for comfort. Welcome to Dubai in July! Yes, this should have been checked, but now we had moved out of the hotel we were stuck and had to sit it out.

At this stage what should have been quiet euphoria, having straddled the great divide from Surrey to downtown Dubai relatively unscathed, was turning into yet another test of one's metal. Far from being great I found myself rattling around the apartment, which was sparsely furnished and, dare I say it, a little inhospitable, with my wondrous purchases eyeing me up and down as if to say 'when will you ever use me?' I couldn't have agreed more. Yes, what was I doing with Waterford Crystal glasses, Kings pattern cutlery, a bone china dinner service and all those cosmetics? It seemed unimaginable that all would eventually be put to very good use and together we would bloom like the desert rose.

Yes, yet again I felt like a prisoner, but this time had no BOAC pals to jolly the situation along and Mike was away for what seemed like an eternity every day. We had no telephone and, in those Stone Age days, there was no radio or television in Dubai. About two weeks after we had moved in, Mike informed me that he was going to Abu Dhabi for the day — a very long day and a very long way. This was to do a recce to ascertain whether it would be feasible for his enormous bitumen road tankers to transverse the route safely because there were no roads at that time, just rolling sand dunes and the occasional subka track. I can testify that it sure was a Desperate Dan sort of ride!

Off he went and I passed the day waiting for his return. It got to about 9pm and I was stiff with fear — where was he? Then there was a knock on the door. 'Hallelujah,' I cried, but it was not Mike. It was his driver who handed me a note from Mike saying he had collapsed on arrival in Abu Dhabi due to heat exhaustion and a lack of salt and would return the next day by plane.

There just had to be a little bit of bulldog spirit lurking underneath this brittle surface of mine to enable me to cope with my first night alone in this desert kingdom, not having a clue as to when I would see Mike again or, for that matter, if I would ever see him again!

It transpired that the journey took over nine hours in temperatures upwards of 40°C. This toxic mix took its toll and heat exhaustion was the result. Now this was a salutary lesson, as the body requires extra salt to withstand these high temperatures and without it is unable to function properly; that, my friends, was the understatement of the year! As a note, in those days we were issued with salt tablets which we were required to take every day over and above our normal intake, to enable the body to keep on an even keel.

Not bad going, two sagas resolved; now surely it would be full steam ahead without any more catastrophes. Life might even settle into some sort of pattern, but I wasn't holding my breath. It would be a question of taking each day as it came, hoping against hope that some progress had been made to enable our new life to fully blossom into that wondrous flower, the desert rose. I thought I might need to hold my breath though!

Still Alive!

There we were at eight weeks into our first year and we were still alive to tell the tale, wonders will never cease. It was July and very, very hot. I now knew why there were hardly any expat women around, as they had all fled to cooler climes. We were gradually getting the low-down on the mysterious workings of this desert kingdom, although it was more through osmosis than being guided around by somebody who had previously trodden the same path. I thought by the time I met anybody in the know I would have melted, fled or died of boredom!

Ali and I were getting to know each other and demarcation lines were gradually being sorted out. It was quite preposterous to think that I was now a 'Mem' and poor Ali was totally at my beck and call. The very first task he was given was to provide us with early morning tea. As you know, no self-respecting English person arises without first partaking in a glorious cup of hot tea, a ritual not to be missed, even in faraway places. Firstly, he had to be taught how to make an English cup of tea, that's one without diluting it with evaporated milk then inundating it with sugar!

The morning of the inauguration of this age old ritual had arrived. We were woken with a knock on the door but Ali did not appear. 'Where are you?' said Mike. The door opened slightly and an arm protruded, holding a tray on which was our tea, but no Ali. Again Mike said, 'Please come in,' with which Ali appeared, shielding his eyes from the bed with his other arm. I dived under the sheets and Mike watched with amusement as Ali gingerly served the tea, I think with his eyes closed, and then he fled. A little cameo we still treasure. This was early morning tea Dubai style!

Then there was the washing and cleaning. We did not possess a washing machine, so all the clothes were thrown into the bath by Ali. The bath was filled with water and the water liberally sprinkled with washing powder, and then he climbed in and proceeded to trample on the clothes. Gee, this was novel, but it was soon apparent that it really was a very clever way of 'doing the washing'. Thus began my descent into total dependence on having a houseboy to be there for my every whim and wish; I can hear Mike saying I have him now — there is one problem though, he answers back!

The cleaning of the apartment was straightforward with just a brush, duster, mop and bucket. Nothing too complicated, as long as I wasn't involved. The most difficult task was cooking. As previously mentioned, a good 'Mem' had to have an all-rounder as a houseboy as, quite naturally, one was judged by the quality of the food that emanated from the kitchen, as if by magic. Blimey, now that was a task that I really wasn't sure whether I would be able to achieve. I could cook, but whether I would be able to teach Ali to cook to my exacting standards (Cordon Bleu, naturally) was another matter.

Before there was any thought of entertaining, we had to meet people, I had to locate the shops and the market, and also had to find out just what Ali's culinary skills were. As you can't cook without produce, the first stop had to be the local market which sold fruit, vegetables, fish and meat. The market was quite large, situated at the head of the Creek on the Deira side, and I was able to go by taxi. Once there, it was really quite daunting.

There was an enormous section for fruit and vegetables, where each trader had a stall. These stalls were slightly vertical with the produce being piled high on shelves that seemingly reached upwards to the skies, with the trader sitting right at the top. To reach the produce he would swing down from a rope which was attached to the ceiling, and to converse with him one got a rick in the neck! The language was no problem though as everyone spoke English. In fact, the choice of fresh fruit and vegetables was quite bewildering as there were so much exotica from Africa, like mangoes, pineapples and pawpaws.

The fish was in another section, where there were rows of marble workstations and burly fishermen who were busy gutting the day's catch which mostly consisted of enormous Hamour fish, somewhat akin to cod, which was very much the staple fish of the Gulf. Everything was awash with water and blood — not a pretty sight. If fish was required for the dinner table then this is where one came; it was definitely no place for the squeamish and was surely light years away from shopping in Sainsbury's.

I could never bring myself to purchase meat because this section was a little like Noah's Ark but on land; all the animals were lined up one by one, all for the chop and pot!

Our first dinner party was getting closer and all I had to do was find a supermarket. I think two existed, one being quite close and called Hassani's. It really was very fusty indeed but seemed to sell the basics that were required to keep body and soul together. There were also large refrigerators stuffed with frozen slabs which purported to be meat, but what sort was anyone's guess as quite often there were power cuts and, once defrosted and then refrozen, these slabs just took on a different shape and sat there quietly waiting to be purchased. In those days, sell by dates were unheard of and the old adage to 'never refreeze anything that had been defrosted' was risible.

We are living proof that sell by dates should be taken with a very large pinch of salt! Together with an equally large gin and tonic!

Fruit and vegetable market, Deira
Image courtesy of Len Chapman, copyright holder

Liquor Licence!

Almost everything was in place to ensure that Apartment 603 was totally shipshape and ready to invite guests but one vital ingredient was missing and that was any form of alcoholic beverage. Yes, it was a strange place, it was possible to obtain a beer or a gin and tonic in a hotel bar but, without a very important piece of paper wondrously called a 'liquor licence', it was impossible to obtain anything for home consumption.

For another little conundrum, we were told that once all the necessary work permits had been processed then Mike would be issued with the said licence, which was all quite mysterious. Technically, not being in possession of this wondrous piece of paper meant that it was illegal to have any alcohol in your possession, even as a 'gift' of a bottle from a chum!

These licences were issued and stamped by the Chief of Police who, in fact, was British. In this way, it meant that no Muslim had to be involved with anything relating to the dreaded alcohol, and consequently the teachings of the Koran were not being compromised and everyone could go on their merry way, both literally and metaphorically. This special piece of paper, once in Mike's sticky fingers, would enable us to go on our merry way too! But where did one go to procure said 'contraband', how much could one buy and at what cost?

It transpired that there were one or two 'liquor shops' in Dubai that were both run by British trading companies. However, they were difficult to find at first because they were literally in disguise as all the outside walls were bricked up and there were no signs on the doors. I suppose it could almost have been compared to hunting for the famous grouse on distant shores, but this Famous Grouse just happened to be in a bottle and, to the uninitiated, could be equally as elusive.

As far as I can remember there were no windows in these establishments, or if there were they were protected by steel bars. This was to prevent the other 99 per cent of Dubai's inhabitants from entering, who would possibly have liked a nice cold beer on a very hot day.

Once inside, a veritable Aladdin's Cave presented itself, a party goer's paradise, and surely there was nothing that one could not buy from the best French champagnes to malt whiskies and a myriad of different makes of beer. In one's wildest dreams this first visit to a Dubai liquor store could never have been imagined, and it was mind blowing to think it was just down the road from the apartment; how wonderfully convenient! Compared with the UK, the prices were extremely low, which made the whole buying experience even better and a little bit naughty, as possibly one shouldn't really be doing this in a Muslim country! There was only one rule and that was you couldn't exceed the monetary amount you had been allotted, which was based on a percentage of one's salary. We quickly got the hang of this buying procedure and after that first visit the 'ship never ran dry'!

Life was now settling into a pattern with Mike leaving at 6.30am and returning at about 2.30pm, six days a week. These were the usual working hours in the Gulf in those days, especially during the summer when it was very hot. We then used to partake of a light lunch, as was our custom in the UK, but gradually realized that this was a little daft because Ali was not being totally utilized as his duties finished after lunch. I was then attempting to cook dinner and, would you believe it, there was no air conditioning in the kitchen. We were also starting to receive invitations to cocktail parties, which always started at 7pm. We then found that we never had time for dinner — oh, what a muddle we got into!

As you will be aware, cocktail nibbles are no substitute for dinner and, with the size of the gin and tonics that were poured and consumed, these evenings took on a very rosy hue indeed, and dinner often fell by the wayside. Don't tell Mother!

That was a small price to pay though as we were slowly meeting people although, as it was still high summer, it was mostly 'bachelors' with the wives still being in the UK or elsewhere, possibly up some mountain or other cooling off, but it was a start and I knew that if I could be patient for a little while longer things should look up. As we still didn't have a telephone it would have been incredibly difficult even making contact with anyone but we were getting to know the lie of the land, such as the fact that every Thursday evening there was a gathering at the Bustan Hotel. The hotel bar was the designated 'watering hole' for most of the expats at a loose end, and was where they congregated to enjoy a beer or two and to catch up on the week's happenings, which no doubt wasn't a lot.

Being such a very small community, nearly all of these people knew of our existence, which was a little unnerving but that was the way things were and something that we were going to have to get used to until we were superseded by another unsuspecting couple who would undergo exactly the same initiation procedure. Like it or loathe it that was how things were.

After this we were scooped up and encouraged to join in the various activities that were on offer – mostly using the hotel swimming pool and playing tennis – but, oh it was so hot, thank goodness we were both sporty and game for anything otherwise we would really have been up a gum tree, confined to barracks, and possibly feeling very sorry for ourselves!

Dubai was no place for bookworms, and I'm not too sure whether you could even buy a book worth reading, but surprise, surprise you could purchase English newspapers that were two days out of date. We had no other means of communication with the outside world, so what was a couple of days between friends. Now, I wonder who has ever heard of anybody so desperate for news that they were prepared to trudge across a sand patch to collect an out of date English newspaper, which incidentally cost a fortune, in temperatures of 40°C? You would possibly have said it must be a madman — maybe you are right!

Apartment 603!

There was a gentle lull in Apartment 603. Ali had got to grips with the early morning schedule, as had Mike, but I was still trying to figure out just how I was going to occupy all those hours from 6.30am until 2.30pm when Mike normally reappeared. Usually, this was the end of his working day and the longed for time when my playmate returned. Am I sounding a little forlorn? Yes, probably, and maybe a little defeatist. From the time of Mike's departure until his return the empty hours stretching before me loomed large and I needed a very fertile imagination to keep my pecker up and my wits about me. Oh, how sad it all was.

As you will be aware, it's jolly hot in the Gulf especially during the summer. To make working conditions somewhat more bearable, most people worked until 2pm. This resulted in a seven-hour working day with no break, and that was six days a week. I, on the other hand, had all the time in the world, but what to do? The odd game of tennis was coming my way but in temperatures of up to 40°C one had to be desperate. The only other activity that one could indulge in without the fear of getting sunstroke was that jolly card game of bridge, and in an attempt to learn this damnable game I repeatedly fell by the wayside.

I was in a total quandary. I needed something to do but was unsure that I was so desperate that I would willingly fall foul of so many of those formidable ladies who lived for the game and, I'm sure, even retired to bed wearing green eye shields.

After due deliberation I decided to give it a whirl and tentatively let slip that, yes, I did play but not too well. Actually, that was a massive understatement because once seated at the bridge table one morning with the cards in my hand, shaking like a proverbial leaf, I realized that I had no real idea as to what my next move should be. When the bidding had reached three 'no trumps' on the opponents' side and I had not responded to any of my partner's bids and could feel her eyes piercing into me, I thought maybe I should take a flying leap, but where to? Under the table was too close for comfort and I supposed dashing out of the door would have rendered me a party pooper! It was more than apparent that I had no clue on God's earth what was going on.

If a morning on my own was bad then this was excruciating and it surely must have reached ten on the Richter scale of one's most terrifying moments. My only joy had to be that I was so bad that they would never invite me again, but I had no doubt that after this encounter they would be convinced that Mike was married to the village idiot. I left feeling very contrite!

I quickly realized that playing card games in the morning with formidable ladies to while away the hours wasn't, and would never be, my idea of fun, so that was a valuable lesson learnt. I was in need of a bona fide occupation fast, but how was I going to find this elusive pimpernel? Divine intervention was most definitely required!

We were getting nearer to obtaining a telephone, which would obviously help my plight, and August was drawing to a close with the 'wives' slowly returning to take up the reigns, organizing everything from coffee mornings to luncheons and really formal dinner parties. You sure needed a fertile imagination to keep the show on the road and your feet on the ground in this place!

We were now receiving quite a few invitations to drinks parties, but I am quite sure that lots of them were from inquisitive people to see whether we would pass muster and also to become acquainted with the General Manager and his wife of the newest company in Dubai. I think we did!

Most of these invitations were very formal, using the same format as for wedding invitations. They were always professionally printed and some, I think, were even embossed. That was our next task as it was quite obvious we had to conform and not let the side down, but where were the printers? Mike managed to get the 'show on the road' and we were soon the proud possessors of 100 very smart formal invitation cards bearing our names 'Mr and Mrs M H T Constable' and 'requests the pleasure of the company of' with spaces to add the whoever to whatever, and at the bottom was our phone number and, of course, 'RSVP'. Actually, this gave me quite a buzz as progress was being made in this social minefield but what I did not bargain for was our very disastrous first dinner party. To this day it makes me want to hang my head in shame as it was so shambolic. It proved the point that sending out smart dinner invitations did not mean that the party would go with a swing, and we had an awful lot to learn if we were going to be able to keep up with the Joneses.

Occasionally there was a handwritten 'RO' at the bottom of the card, but could I figure this out? No, it took forever, it was a little like communicating in shorthand, and I eventually discovered it meant 'Regrets Only'. This was like learning a whole new language and another anomaly was that the envelopes were always addressed to Mrs Michael Constable. I used to think it was very strange that they were only inviting me and not Mike. It was some time before I learnt that this was the form in polite circles. Yes, even in this desert kingdom the memsahibs were sticklers for protocol.

1970 was just at the tail end of the Raj and East Africa was becoming a little tricky so consequently quite a few expats from East Africa were posted to Dubai. Some of these people worked for Smith Mackenzie in East Africa and were transferred to Gray Mackenzie in Dubai. Goodness, these memsahibs were real Kahais; they could teach new recruits like me a thing or two and frighten one to death into the bargain.

Everything was so incredibly formal. One custom was to call on a new arrival to introduce oneself which, in fact, was a very civilized custom but it could be a terrifying experience for a young wife, like me, to be confronted in such a manner. Actually, without telephones there was no other way of making contact other than smoke signals, but sometimes I think they were secretly being nosey. If one was not at home, the houseboy would probably invite them in and offer a suitable beverage; consequently it was not unheard of to arrive home to find some formidable woman occupying your favourite armchair waiting for your arrival — what a fright that was! Then it was up to you to make a good account of yourself! It really helped if your lineage dated back to the Doomsday Book and a hint of blue could be detected in your veins; snobbery was rife in those days.

Another must that had to be addressed was whether there were any hairdressers in this place, as I was utterly incapable of fixing my own hair. As we still knew very few people it was difficult to find out, but along from the apartment was a little hairdressing salon where an enormous fat Indian lady, with long streaky black hair, sat behind a counter with her equally fat son beside her. Not exactly a good advert, but I was desperate so I braved it. She pointed to a stepladder leading up to the second floor but, for one fleeting moment, I thought she was going to tell me to shin up a rope to reach this secret place. Once there I found myself in a salon, Bombay style, where a young Indian hairdresser was waiting to attend to my every need. Mercifully my hair didn't fall out and we soon became good pals, and for quite a while she was the best coiffeur I knew this side of Bond Street.

Once again, the point was proved that adaptability was surely the name of the game!

Curry Lunches!

I think I can safely say that we were able to give ourselves a little pat on the back as all was well in Apartment 603. This well-being came about because we had started receiving invitations to the young bachelors' curry lunch parties, which were held most Thursday lunchtimes and hosted by the boys from the Banking and Accountancy fraternity. We were quite literally guaranteed to be propelled into the weekend at breakneck speed and quite often rendered rudderless, like a Molotov cocktail. Thinking about it, that's probably what we were offered to drink!

Being with these boys always brought a smile to one's face as they were bright, very funny, always irreverent and their jokes were quite preposterous. At that time, making the best of what was on offer in Dubai wasn't always easy, but they usually found a way!

Much to my joy we then discovered that on Thursday nights at the Bustan Hotel there was what could only be described as a 'hop'.

The first time we were guided there by some of the worse for wear bachelors as those curry lunches carried on for hours and hours but, by now, Mike and I were going with the flow too and really didn't bat an eyelid. I'm quite positive this would never have happened in the UK — a young married woman constantly being surrounded by young single men, and maybe being a little flattered by all the attention, perish the thought! Oh, the memory of it all.

We were not too sure as to what to expect on our first visit to the Bustan but I suppose it might have been akin to finding oneself in the kingdom of heaven as we exploded into a large ornate room, the likes of which we had never seen before, with the chairs being upholstered in red velvet and heavy velvet drapes complete with sways at the windows; how plush. I was to discover that the owners of the hotel were Lebanese and this type of décor was very much their style. I thought it was a touch of Versailles!

It sure seemed at odds with the young blades who were there enjoying a few beers and maybe, if lucky, a hop around the dance floor. Mind you, there was one mighty problem — dancing partners were thin on the ground as there were few single girls in Dubai back then. I have to add that it was, and still is, forbidden in certain Arab countries to cohabit if you were not married; it may be a little more lenient now in some quarters, but in those days it really makes me shudder to think what might have happened to the 'guilty parties' if they were rumbled!

The very first time we went to the Thursday night 'hop' was a total amazement because of the number of people that seemed to be crammed into the room. They were all expats, bachelor boys who were hoping to find a single girl to whirl around the dance floor and lonely husbands whiling away the time until their wives returned from summer leave. We found it quite extraordinary as so many of them knew who we were; how was that? We soon discovered it was because we were the newest couple in town – no, it wasn't fame – and it emphasized just how small Dubai was at that time.

At long last we were to discover just how this town operated as we were taken under the wing of the old hands who knew a thing or two about survival. Soothing words came my way from various summer bachelors of, 'You will be fine once our wives return,' and 'It won't be long now, they will get you organized, so "chin up"!' I suppose it was our version of 'carry on regardless', but it was an enormous breakthrough and a relief to see lots of young, happy faces. Mind you, that might have been because it was Dubai's equivalent of happy hour down at the pub and the next day, Friday, was a holiday.

Friday was the day of rest and prayer if you were a Muslim and a day of hijinks if you weren't. I think for us there was much more emphasis on 'play' and why not indeed; we were like birds whose wings had been clipped, desperately trying to flee the confines of the 'nest', which for us was the apartment.

After this introduction to the Bustan Hotel for evening entertainment, we then discovered that it could provide daytime entertainment too as it had a lovely swimming pool and two or three tennis courts, so we now had a 'Friday' bolt hole. 'Alhamdulillah', wonders will never cease!

There was just one stumbling block. We had to forget that the temperatures were upside of 40°C, but it was either die of boredom in the apartment or from sunstroke at the pool, so there was no contest really. And to think we hardly donned a sun hat, let alone slather ourselves with sun oil. We would be for the high jump now in today's politically correct world.

Little did we know that this was the real beginning of a far, far different way of life than the one we had left behind, and one we would never have imagined possible a few months earlier before we were hurled onto this roller coaster, and I think, yes, maybe we were warming to the theme.

Other people we met during those hot hazy days were some of the young officers who were stationed at Sharjah, about 20 kilometres away over the desert. They were either from RAF Sharjah or a small British military contingent stationed alongside, and then there were the dashing, mostly British, young officers from the Trucial Oman Scouts, affectionately known as the TOS. To receive an invitation to one of their curry lunches was deemed to have arrived, and the first time Mike and I had the honour I nearly fainted with excitement!

The TOS were based in Sharjah and it was primarily a desert based regiment that had initially been called the Oman Levies. The bulk of the regiment was comprised of Bedouins recruited mainly from Abu Dhabi, and the young officers were seconded from the British Army and were, in the main, from mounted British regiments. Without exception they seemed to revel in their new found status of a budding Lawrence of Arabia.

The line from Noel Coward's song, 'Mad dogs and Englishmen go out in the midday sun', could well have been penned with these pukka young chaps in mind. I am sure though that when he wrote this ditty he had no real idea of how true his words would resonate with these passionate young chaps who truly embraced this different type of soldiering, loving the desert, happily replacing horses with camels as their mounts, and generally having a true empathy with their men and conversing in Arabic when necessary. Although once in the Officers' Mess normal service was always resumed. They were officers and gentlemen through and through.

Trip to Abu Dhabi!

Mike arrived home to say he had to go to Abu Dhabi to check on the progress of his bitumen supply depot and would I like to go too? Now that was an offer not to be missed, or so I thought!

The intention was to leave in a couple of days, very early in the morning, to make sure that the bulk of the journey was completed in the somewhat cooler hours of the day. I duly packed; obviously I had in mind that I was going to visit a mysterious exotic kingdom. Why was that? Because it was a little tricky getting there, although as the crow flies it was only about 100 kilometres. In those far off days there were no roads in the conventional sense, only subka tracks weaving their way perilously over the sand dunes. I was told it would feel like driving over corrugated iron, extremely uncomfortable and by the end of the journey one's kidneys would be crying out for help!

Our driver duly arrived at 6am and we set off. This time I knew that those little Dior numbers would not be appropriate even if I was to meet the Queen of Sheba on arrival!

We drove away from the apartment and were early enough to admire the beautiful sunrise over the Al Maktoum Bridge as we travelled along a few kilometres of tarmac road before hitting the desert track. My initiation into desert bashing was about to begin!

We bounced, swerved and thudded over the dunes with camels galloping all around us. Yes, I was left in no doubt that we were on our way. Was this really going to be an experience not to be missed, I wondered, as from the outset it really was so incredibly uncomfortable, even in a Mercedes. It was so very slow, and how the driver knew which direction he was going in I will never know. Perhaps he had a compass, as obviously there were not any road signs in the desert! It was most definitely turning into a mystery tour without any magic. It did not take long before the novelty had worn off but obviously there was no turning back as we were rocked and rolled from one sand dune to the next.

Eventually, after what seemed an eternity, we spied a sight for sore eyes over the horizon. Yes, it was the border post; thank God, a sign that we were getting closer to our destination. Now this border post was very strange indeed as it was in the middle of nowhere and consisted of a hut, which was manned by a border guard. Attached to the hut was a barrier which was always open except at prayer time between 6pm and 7pm when you had to wait. Passports were presented and duly stamped – quite bizarre – after which we were on our way.

As we approached the island of Abu Dhabi we hit a tarmac road and, oh joy of joys, our kidneys were saved from any more poundings, but I was not too sure how the head felt! Then there was yet another border post which had to be negotiated where the passports were required to be presented once again. This was at the entrance to the bridge which had to be crossed to gain access to the island itself which, in fact, was the main commercial centre of Abu Dhabi. After all the anticipation it sure didn't look too much like Shangri-La. What a day this was turning out to be. The journey from Dubai to Abu Dhabi had taken approximately seven hours. It might have been quicker on a camel!

We reached the Guest House where we were staying, which really was more like a large prefab with a corrugated iron roof situated in a nice patch of sand; even our apartment was more exotic than this, and that was saying something. I was to discover that these guest houses always had very attentive staff to cater for one's every whim and wish as they were normally frequented by the bachelors, or visiting 'firemen' as chaps from London were fondly referred too. I quickly discovered this because I ended up being stuck in the place all day, and once again there wasn't a playmate in sight. So yes, I did wonder why I had been so pleased to be invited along; another little blunder!

Abu Dhabi, in those days, was extremely small but it had a magnificent cornice which had been built alongside the lagoon. On one side there were banks, a few shops and one hotel – I think it was called the Oasis – and on the other a promenade that was used by the inhabitants to stroll along in the cool of the evening. Unfortunately, the Guest House was too far away to take advantage of this facility and it was August after all!

Mike suggested that the driver took me to Al Ain for the day which is an oasis inland from Abu Dhabi, as if I hadn't had enough of desert journeys, but it was the best he could do.

Actually it was more like hitting a Wild West town. It consisted of a dusty main street with a few shops and coffee shops on either side; no cowboys though, but plenty of camels lolling around together with their Bedouin owners. The striking difference was the abundance of greenery together with masses of date laden palm trees. After the dusty desert it was a joy to behold and it soon became clear why it was an oasis and held in such esteem by the Bedouins as for them it must have been like arriving in paradise.

Little did I know though that disaster was lurking around the corner as I was bitten by a giant spider on my foot which proceeded to swell at an alarming rate. There were no doctors in Al Ain, only camel doctors and that wouldn't do, so once back in Abu Dhabi something had to be done.

My first encounter with a doctor in foreign parts was about to happen but nothing prepared me for this rendezvous. Dr Martin was a Scot and had been in Abu Dhabi for years. He delighted in the nickname 'Remy Martin', was utterly charming, gave me a jab and a stiff brandy, and declared I would surely live to fight another day. I was somewhat reassured that he was so optimistic but at the time I had my doubts!

After three days we flew back to Dubai in a Fokka Friendship, the smallest plane I had ever seen let alone flown in. To this day, I'm not sure which was more frightening, charging over sand dunes at a rate of knots or experiencing flying in something akin to a kite!

After that little 'outward bound' exercise I was extremely pleased to be back 'home'; now that really was an admission, or was it about the devil one knew?

Horrendous Journey!

I had just about recovered from my 'educational' trip to Abu Dhabi. If nothing else the experience made me appreciate Dubai a little more than before we set off and that was really saying something. Fancy having to endure that pantomime to find myself actually uttering those words.

Safely back in Dubai it was so very hard to imagine that just across those sand dunes lay Abu Dhabi, a small desert kingdom that really did seem a world away from anywhere.

I now had renewed vigour and, as Mike had suggested, we should brave it and have our first dinner party. I readily agreed. Having survived that monumental drive across the desert I was up for anything, well almost!

Compared to the last few tortuous days this should be a walk in the park — I was in for a bit of a surprise! This new life of mine was turning into a veritable assault course and there were obstacles to be negotiated around every corner. Surely there must be some sort of medal ceremony to look forward to? When and where, that's what I wanted to know!

Mike suggested that it would, perhaps, be kind to invite two 'summer bachelors' whom he had met through business for dinner. This didn't sound too onerous; in fact, it could be a dummy run for parties to come, what a splendid idea.

A date was set and I began organizing a menu but trying to locate even basic ingredients in those far off days could be like looking for a needle in a haystack; actually that task might have been somewhat easier.

My fears were soon confirmed; Ali did not possess any finer culinary skills but thought he knew it all, and who was I to disagree. Between us we set the table with my finest purchases from London for their first appearance 'on the stage'. It really was quite exciting.

Ali assured me that he had everything under control and if I was going to be the perfect 'Mem' I had to be relaxed about the whole situation. Oh dear, it soon became very clear that I was going to regret that decision.

Our guests duly arrived and it soon transpired that neither of them were a bundle of fun; in fact, they hardly spoke a word. The only thing Mike could think of doing to rectify this situation was to ask Ali to make the drinks stronger and stronger in the hope that these two would become a little more garrulous. Ali was struggling in the kitchen and I was on the verge of extreme hysteria, when one of these learned gentlemen fell through his chair. It had collapsed, not him, I hasten to add.

Mike and I nearly died of fright at this spectacle of one collapsed chair and one guest sprawled over the floor. Should I run for it, find the smelling sorts or grab yet another stiff gin?

Dinner pronto, I thought. Bad move. This was to be Ali's moment of culinary glory, in fact his finest hour, so what did he do? Our first course was fish of some description with tartar sauce, which he assured me was a doddle to make.

Once our guests had been seated we waited for Ali's appearance. In retrospect, it was to be like a game of charades unfolding before our eyes as suddenly, without any preamble, he charged through the swinging door, shrouded in a gigantic white apron, shoeless and carrying an enormous tray which he plonked on the floor and proceeded to serve dinner from there.

What was I to do? Actually it was somewhat late to do anything except watch in horror as this cameo unfolded and silently wish I was sitting at somebody else's dinner table. The fish looked passable but the tartar sauce somewhat strange. It transpired that it had been made with flour, cold water and, I think for good measure, a large slug of vinegar. It's a wonder we didn't all choke to death.

At this stage I was still trying to act like a proper 'Mem' and pretend everything was fine and all these antics were quite normal in our household. Even in their inebriated state these two chaps must have thought Mike and I were ten parts barmy!

On reflection we were fortunate that our guests had consumed so much whisky that I don't think they had a clue as to what they were eating or drinking but at least they were talking! The rest of the meal was passable but I think we all retired with monumental indigestion and me with a very red face!

I really wasn't too sure after that episode if I would, or could, ever redeem myself or be able to transform Ali into any sort of cook at all. Afterwards, he told me that he was very adept at cooking 'mutton grabs' which was a whole sheep on a spit and a speciality of the locals. Now that would have been fine if we had been living in a Bedouin tent in the middle of the desert.

Somehow between us we had to up our game. But how? It took a while to recover from this episode but it was another learning curve, and obviously trying to school Ali into becoming a passable Cordon Bleu star was going to be a near impossibility — a distant dream. It definitely would be a challenge, one I don't think either of us was up to at that moment in time! Although, I thought I might just take time out and show him how to make tartar sauce!

So that was another hurdle over. The experience had been somewhat akin to being entered for the Derby but actually only being fit for the Donkey Derby, and I think even a three-legged donkey would have overtaken us.

What a dismal performance, three out of ten, must try harder! For the foreseeable future we should stick to accepting invitations not giving them, and maybe check out the local takeaways!

Jan riding a camel
Trucial Oman Scouts, Sharjah

Monumental Flop!

We were somewhat bewildered as to why our first attempt at formal entertaining was a monumental flop, especially as I believed that I was a good cook and hostess. Ah, but that was in leafy Surrey not in this far away desert kingdom where available ingredients left a lot to be desired, together with a cook who didn't know one end of a wooden spoon from another and me, the hostess, flapping around like a demented dervish.

Not the most ideal of recipes for a flawless dinner party, no wonder I felt as if I had just presided over the dinner party from hell!

I was able to put this disastrous episode behind me as the 'summer wives' were beginning to return and I was being swept up by these 'gals' who were all seasoned expat wives, par excellence.

I was soon being shown the ropes and at long last was introduced to the wondrous souks that nestled alongside the Creek, included in tennis and swimming parties, and also introduced to Friday picnics up the coast in a little fishing village called Ajman. It was a question of making the best of what was on offer and these girls knew how to do this in spades. Mind you, they had had a lot of practise.

My first sortie was to the Gold Souk. What an amazing experience, and to this day I still marvel that such a place exists in the world. The souk was actually a narrow road heading off from the Creek that was crammed with tiny shops on both sides all selling gold jewellery.

The shop windows were festooned from top to toe with gaudy gold that looked as if it would have been more at home in a Christmas cracker, being very yellow and bright. I discovered that this was because it was 22 or even 24 carat, and adored by the Arabs and Indians, normally being bought as part of the dowries for their weddings. The designs and colour were definitely not understated but that was how they liked it; if you can afford it flaunt it, that's what I say.

I digress. We were walking down this narrow road, jostling for space with donkeys being led by their masters, that was packed to the gunnels with goods, maybe exotic spices that had probably just been unloaded from a dhow which had recently sailed in from as far away as Zanzibar, or fruits from East Africa. Being utterly mesmerized by the sight, sounds and smell of this place was the moment that my love affair began, not only with Arabia but with gold! A love affair that has stood the test of time!

It was hard not to be seduced by the amazement of this street. Maybe there were fifty little shops, or dukas as they were known locally, with the owners all vying for the same custom and all selling identical pieces of jewellery. How could they all survive as competition was obviously fierce? Everywhere one looked there was gold twinkling in the shop windows and one almost needed sunglasses because it was so dazzling. It really was hard to appreciate that so much wealth was crammed into this understated street. Bond Street it was not, but the atmosphere was unrivalled.

I discovered that nearly all the jewellers were from either Jordan or Syria. They were very astute business people and I expect that they all slept in their shops on a little mezzanine floor at the back, in their home away from home. On reflection, these shops hardly every closed except for Friday morning prayers, when no doubt they prayed that there would be plenty of business that evening, as Friday is a holiday in all Muslim countries.

This first visit was like the opening of Pandora's box, albeit it a golden box, and somehow it explained so much. In essence, this little street was Arabia in a nut shell with its toxic smell of exotic spices, and the hustle and bustle of the coolies going about their business, either leading laden donkeys to their next destination or carrying a multitude of goods precariously balanced on their heads. The Chai boys offered sweet tea and the patrons tried to entice customers into their shops to purchase some amazing piece of gaudy gold, costing a king's ransom.

Needless to say, the girls had found a way round the dilemma of desperately wanting a gold necklace but not being up for the gaudy stuff. A very astute vendor was quick on the uptake and realized there was a market for more refined pieces, usually 18 carat, which were normally made in Italy. That was when Damascus Jewellers was established as the best address in the souk, a must for ladies that shop!

Naturally I couldn't get back quickly enough to tell Mike where I had been, and that I had the great idea that he should come with me next time — I wonder why! Subsequently, I spent many a happy hour bartering with, was it Ali or Mohammed, because out of all the streets and alleyways in Dubai this was the one place where dreams really did come true. Actually, I think it was Dubai's answer to the Kingdom of Heaven!

Raining Gold!

I never thought I would be as thrilled as I was to have found a 'glitzy' shopping street where one could loiter to one's heart's content, albeit competing for walking space with donkeys with their vast loads of exotica from the East.

They were slowly meandering along the rutted sand road together with coolies dashing hither and yon, well-dressed European ladies and also the burka brigade, all with their eyes glued to the gaudy window displays dreaming of waking up in the morning being adorned in gold! I think it would be fair to say that the street was raining gold!

To say I was awestruck would be an understatement; it was love at first sight. I was led to believe that diamonds were a girl's best friend but I had a monumental change of mind.

Entering this little backstreet obviously couldn't be compared to entering Harrods – there were no super tall doormen clad in their distinctive green uniforms, doffing their top hats to one and all, red carpets or splendid chandeliers – just scruffy little men dashing hither and yon going about their business.

This was serious jewellery shopping, par excellence, Dubai style. For many, entering this golden heaven must have been akin to stepping into paradise. Just breathing in the atmosphere was an aphrodisiac in itself but to actually purchase a talisman of gold was enough to make the most blasé of shoppers swoon with delight and maybe pass out into the bargain. It was a golden moment to be treasured.

I was now definitely warming to Dubai, and little did I know what other delights were awaiting me in the labyrinth of alleyways that made up downtown Deira. Next, I was introduced to the Spice Souk which ran adjacent to the main road that ran alongside the Creek, where dhows were moored. Deckhands and coolies were always to be seen working frantically loading and unloading the ships' cargoes with the coolies' carts being loaded with great sacks of spices from distant shores, like India, Kenya and maybe Zanzibar, then to be trundled along the alleyways that made up the souk to their destinations. Not surprisingly the souk always had a pungent smell, the air being filled with exquisite aromas of Eastern spices, a curry cook's dream. In those days, many of the spices were unknown to us, as yet, not having reached European shores.

Yes, this was another walk into the unknown and into the past as surely this little corner of Dubai hadn't changed for many a moon. Just after the Spice Souk one turned into another small passage which also ran adjacent to the Creek. It had shops on either side with everything being crammed in up to the gunnels. This time the walkway was quite narrow and consequently there was no room for roaming donkeys. Along with enormous sacks of colourful spices, such as yellow turmeric, red chilli powder, orange curry powder, cloves, peppercorns and cinnamon there were mountains of metal cooking pots and utensils that were all big enough to cook giant curries or rice to go with their wonderful mutton grabs. This passage surely must have been the forerunner of Habitat as it stocked everything for dining, Arab style.

One usually found the shopkeepers lolling at the back of their little shops, really more like holes in the wall, patiently waiting for custom, swatting the flies that were buzzing around and fanning themselves to ward off the stifling heat. Surely this was a hard way to earn a living but what else was there to do. These shopkeepers were mostly from afar, possibly Persia, India or Pakistan, and consequently they had to make a go of things but, perhaps, they were better off in this tiny little corner of the world than from whence they came. This was something one would never know, but in my book they sure deserved ten out of ten for tenacity and optimism.

My next foray was to the Textile Souk, another delight awaiting an eager shopper. This street was in the hinterland of the souk, and it was no wonder I had to be taken there in the first instance by those in the know. This quarter was entirely made up of shops selling material and, surprise, they all stocked the same glorious gaudy cloth that we Europeans would only have considered buying to make a fancy dress outfit. Surely we must have been missing something?

These materials were mostly imported from China but there were one or two exceptions. A beady eyed and seasoned souker had spied bolts of Liberty fabric in one shop and bolts of the best worsted material that the UK could offer in another. Then there were bolts of the bright fine white cotton material that was used to make the Arab dishdasha and its black counterpart which was used to make the ladies' abayas.

The Indian ladies were catered for too, as there were wonderful sari materials in all colours of the rainbow sitting on the shelves all vying with each other in their splendour and begging to be transformed into an exotic dress or sari to grace the next 'state occasion'.

This hadn't quite been a walk on the wild side but the sights and sounds of this little corner of Dubai together with the sun sinking over the skyline, the mullahs calling the faithful to prayer and the smell of the shawarmas cooking on every corner made one's heart want to sing. At that moment in time, what more could one have wished for.

Actually, this downtown foray had thrown up a little conundrum: where did I find a tailor pronto? Having done that, I would be able to indulge my fantasies to my heart's content. My goodness, it was now clear I had another objective in life!

Oh, another thought, I wondered if there was a Vogue pattern book lurking somewhere. No, not over the rainbow but under a counter in one of these dusty emporiums. Seemingly, this part of the world had many surprises up its sleeve, so fingers crossed.

On that note I meandered home alongside the Creek, dreaming of many more happy shopping days in my newly adopted 'shopping precinct' with the sun exquisitely setting in the west, creating an amber hue across the sky. My goodness, what an unexpectedly happy outing that had been.

Great Surprise!

We had now been in Dubai for four and a half months and I think it was time for a little reflection. Much to my great surprise I had weathered the initial storm and if I was at all honest with myself I was secretly enjoying the challenge, but obviously wouldn't tell that to all and sundry.

It had been such a monumental learning curve that trying to describe my life now compared to how it had been to the folks back home would be virtually impossible; actually, most people would have had difficulty even comprehending 'my tale'. Maybe they would think I was suffering from delusions, illusions or a monumental bout of sunstroke, who knows!

As I have detailed, with every passing day I had managed to fit another little piece into this jigsaw puzzle that I was presented with on my arrival in Dubai those few months ago, and the picture now looked reasonably promising. Yes, I think with continued perseverance and a dogged temperament all might be well.

Although I was not exactly overly occupied I was managing to sort my diary out a little. I was now going down to the sailing club most afternoons although it was still exceedingly hot, but the temperature in or by the water was a little more bearable.

As previously mentioned, this really was an all-male domain except when a BOAC crew were stopping over and then there might, just might, be the occasional air hostess to keep me company. I got used to this situation and was always grateful when burly soldiers offered to rig the boat for me — feminine guiles generally paid off.

Actually, I cannot recall ever having met any military personnel before these encounters, which was an education in itself. I think the first 'boys' I met were from the Scots Guards stationed at Sharjah which was about 20 kilometres up the road. They were only too pleased to escape from their hot and dusty desert prison for a few hours.

It sure was difficult to know how to react in their presence and I am in no doubt they must have felt the same but, after the usual British stand-off, we settled into a comfortable regime. I got to know one or two of these chaps quite well; yes, they were tough guys but also family men, who missed home as much as me. But much more than that they were brave as I was quietly to discover, as one or two were actually attached to the SAS, and they don't come stronger or braver than that.

As time passed by we enjoyed a gentle camaraderie whilst also having fun sailing. Thank goodness I was a proficient sailor because it sure saved the day with the wind in my hair and the sun on my back. I would happily sail down the Creek under the Al Maktoum Bridge and past the moored dhows for hours on end and nobody seemed to bat an eyelid — even in those days Dubai was somewhat liberal, especially as I was only wearing a bikini, and it was a wonder I wasn't had up for inciting the natives! 'Bragging again!' I can hear you saying. Not really but please be reminded I was only 27 after all!

Now I had discovered the souks and found a tailor, oh boy. I was madly buying up the Textile Souk and would be had up for loitering if I wasn't too careful. These little forays usually took place in the early evening when the sun was going down and the souks were buzzing with people, mostly Pakistani and Indian coolies who were there to partake of their dinner.

Cooking smells were everywhere and curry permeated the air. The whole place was filled with wonder, anticipation and rumbling stomachs, and it was there that I first encountered shawarmas, those giant like skewers that were either impaled with slivers of chicken or lamb and were cooked by rotating them in front of giant charcoal burners — oh the wonder of it all.

To partake of my first shawarma was amazing — it seemed to be stuffed full of Eastern promise; an exotic tasty bite, especially when washed down with a glass of fresh orange juice.

This was a tasting experience one could never have imagined existed in the whole wide world – pure magic – and even today the most seasoned of soukers probably drool in remembrance of their very first encounter with this rolled up sandwich. Surely it was a little piece of Eastern promise, to be enjoyed 'on the go'!

Now that experience was coupled with having my first dishdasha made, wearing it to a cocktail party and abandoning my little Paris numbers.

Was I becoming a little liberated all those miles away from home and throwing caution to the wind or actually beginning to turn into a 'little Arab' and embracing this strange desert kingdom which was now my home, for the foreseeable future, called Dubai. I wonder!

Bur Dubai Abra Station
Image courtesy of Marian Ball, copyright holder

Creek Side, Dubai!

I would never have thought that our newly acquired abode at Apartment 603, The Almulla Building, Creekside, Dubai would ever have been considered 'home' but it just goes to show how wrong one can be. Although it was a brand new building and at first sight not at all welcoming, the prospect of ever calling it home seemed far from our thoughts. How wrong one can be. Given a little time it came up trumps and did us proud.

The building was set adjacent to the Creek with the dhows and their occupants being our closest neighbours, as one would say, just over the road. I sure don't think I could ever have borrowed a pound of sugar from these neighbours but maybe a goat on the hoof, what an intriguing thought. I am quite sure they would have cooked it for me too!

Outwardly the building was hardly attractive; it appeared to be built from something akin to breeze blocks in unforgiving battleship grey and was surely built to last. Under normal circumstances it would not have warranted a second glance but these were early days in Dubai as far as construction was concerned and, at that time, there was no hint of the building boom that would be unleashed a few years hence. In Wild West terms, the 'gold rush' had not yet begun!

The building's saving grace was its imposing entrance decked out in marble with no expense spared and vast steps leading up to the lifts. Alongside the lifts lay the farash's quarters, which was actually a hole in the wall. In a more upmarket environment he would have had the grand title of 'Doorman' and been resplendent in a smart uniform but this was Dubai so his attire – yes, you have guessed it – was a dishdasha and his name was Mohammed — what a surprise.

He was employed by the owner, Mohammed Almulla, to be his 'eyes and ears' and what a good job he did. Information-wise he must have been worth his weight in gold!

As we were soon to discover, our neighbours were garnered from far and wide being a veritable United Nations, including British, Pakistanis, Indians, Lebanese, Syrians, Jordanians and Americans; what a mix. As they were all in Dubai on business, they mostly spoke English with only a few exceptions. It should be pointed out that in those days English was the language of choice in the business community.

How could one be neighbourly under these circumstances? That was a conundrum. We were all very polite to each other when meeting in the lift whilst going about our business but that was the sum total of any interaction.

This stiff upper lip approach needed jazzing up, or so we thought, and consequently Mike and I had a bright idea to invite the ones that we could communicate with to a little soirée. Gosh we were so daft — it never crossed our minds that their tipple might just be water or fruit juice; just how naive could one be.

The initial exercise proved quite easy. We invited the guy on the top floor, who turned out to be a Scot and was the General Manager of Almulla's Construction Company, another British couple, then Indians who had come up from Aden and were running a very successful trading company, and also a very fine Lebanese gentleman who was with a Lebanese catering company. These were just a few on our 'hit list'.

The evening duly arrived and whilst we were awaiting the first guests there was a power cut — what a catastrophe. Mike ended up banging on people's doors, candle in hand, to be met by men wearing only underpants, too hot and breathless to speak as the heat was truly unbearable at maybe 40-45°C (not funny). So that put paid to what we thought was a very good idea, and our 'breaking the ice' party would have to be put on hold.

The outcome though was most unexpected as the Scottish guy on the top floor was undeterred by a little heat and hurtled down the stairs behind Mike to claim his Scotch. Whilst with us he said he needed a secretary and would I be interested? I hadn't had such a good proposition in ages, and there and then a deal was struck.

They say every cloud has a silver lining and who would have thought that for what started out as such a monumental flop the evening should have had such an amazing ending, for me at least, but I wasn't too sure about my new boss because he had no idea just what he had let himself in for.

I was invited down to see the office the following day. I say 'down' because I could have rolled out of bed and flopped into the typist's chair with ease as the office was just three floors below, on the first floor of this illustrious building.

Mohammed Almulla was a man of many talents; in fact, he owned a construction company and also a trading company. I was assigned to a dingy office in the back apartment which was home to the construction company and, for some unknown reason, also home to lots of Indian clerks, all busy tapping away at calculators. This was a little like a scene from a James Bond movie but I sure wasn't going to be a match for Pussy Galore!

The boss's office was duly located and, on entering, there was a desk on the left on which stood the largest typewriter I had ever seen — it was an electric IBM. In those days, it was state of the art but, oh dear, I was only used to the 'steam' variety. I stared on in horror. How was I ever going to make that thing come to life let alone make it write a letter? To me it looked as if it had just landed from outer space — oh my God, should I make a dash for it now?

The boss's office was straight ahead through a glass petition — horror of horrors, he would be able to watch my every move. So this hole in the wall was to be my new home from 8am to midday, six days a week. In Dubai parlance this was called progress.

I elected to start the following Saturday and was up bright and early, all set for my new challenge. Having run the gauntlet through the office where all the Indians were focused on their calculators, I retreated behind the IBM. There was no sign of the boss so I thought I'd better try and become acquainted with my new electric friend or, more to the point, enemy.

I will be honest; I had no idea on God's earth how to make the bloody thing work. Whatever I prodded or did there was no sign of life; even standing on my head didn't work! I was paralysed with fright and when the boss asked me in for dictation I nearly fainted because I had omitted to explain that my shorthand left a lot to be desired and only if he dictated slowly would I be able to cope!

With the dictation over, I retreated to my position behind the monster becoming more and more frantic because I couldn't get it to fire up. In the end, I had to admit defeat and explained that obviously the typewriter was broken and needed fixing before play could begin!

A mechanic eventually appeared on the scene to declare in a very loud voice, 'No wonder it won't work, it's not plugged in!' I hung my head in shame and realized I had to make amends swiftly and get these letters typed in double-quick time. Yes, there was another problem — once fired up I couldn't control the machine, it kept running away with me with the letters dashing and dancing all over the page. What was I to do? This did seem like such a good idea a few days ago but I now wasn't too sure!

How Awesome!

How awesome, to think that after such a short time I had found something gainful to do during the mornings, or should I really say I was quite astonished that anybody should want to hire me as their secretary or even imagine that I might be an asset in their office. Maybe they had just experienced a monumental lapse of judgement because I couldn't really have been the best of the bunch, or could I?

My new found boss and I quickly came to an understanding which was definitely fortuitous for me otherwise I wouldn't have lasted a minute. Why was that, you may be asking. Well I suppose it can be attributed to 'Sod's Law'. After having endured four months of what can only be described as intense boredom living in this desert wilderness, wondering just what I had done to find myself in this position, my life seemed to have done an about turn, and I was actually gainfully occupied and not twiddling my thumbs.

Mike and I had suddenly found ourselves catapulted onto the cocktail party circuit where I also found my boss. This turned out to be a very merry merry-go-round, the likes of which was enough to addle the brain and, on occasions, render one a little unsteady on the feet.

As I now had to be on parade at 8 o'clock every morning, bright-eyed and bushy-tailed behind my typewriter, there was no time for a lie-in. My life had suddenly taken off like a proverbial rocket, but what direction it was going in was a matter to be determined at a later date. Suffice to say, myself and I were on the move!

Why were these invitations arriving on the proverbial doormat thick and fast? Was it because the summer recess was deemed to be over and it was necessary to fly the flag on behalf of 'your' company?

Let me explain, in those days in Dubai the only way to become acquainted with people operating in the business community was to meet them at social gatherings. These 'parties' also enabled the attendees to quietly size up the opposition from a business point of view and, possibly more importantly, to check out who was new in town and who you thought looked like a jolly couple who would help to keep what was a very hectic social scene proceeding full steam ahead with vim and vigour.

I know you will be thinking that the heat obviously takes its toll on everyone sooner rather than later; maybe, but not quite. Other than social gatherings, there was no other way of meeting people as in those days there were no clubs, bars or pubs where one could socialize or just pass the time of day over a 'pint'.

How then were the guest lists drawn up? In fact, all British companies, and possibly a few non-British, were registered at the Political Agency, together with a list of names of their expatriate personnel. In those days, Dubai was a protectorate, part of the Trucial Oman States, hence it had a political agency and not an embassy, and it was there that the dreaded lists of 'Number Ones' were correlated.

You will wonder just what I am on about; well it was very necessary to grasp the great mystery of just how a list of guests for a said cocktail party was drawn up. Obviously I had no idea as to why an invitation would come winging in from one particular company and not another, but these gatherings were all about making useful business contacts and being able to put a face to a name. Yes, it was networking Dubai style, a tried and tested well-oiled machine.

I was soon to discover, quite brutally it must be said, as to how all this worked. One day a chum phoned — yes, we now had a phone, definitely an improvement on smoke signals! Well, I say a chum, we were all wives in this social melting pot, obviously trying to make our own mark but only being able to do so when we were invited along with our husbands.

Well on this occasion, this much more socially experienced lady informed me that she was engaged on that particular evening and she would not be seeing us, wherever this was, as Mike was not a Number One. In other words, this particular party was for heads of companies only. Quite naturally I was mortified as, ironically, Mike was in Dubai setting up the Bitumen Supply Company, which was jointly owned by Shell and BP. Why on earth didn't the powers that be – I really mean the people who produced these dreaded lists – know? One seemed to be at everyone's mercy and navigating these social minefields was to become quite an art.

So that was another mystery revealed about the wondrous goings on in Dubai all those moons ago but, in retrospect, it was a very clever way of testing the temperature of the water before jumping in. It was 'de rigueur' to be seen at these parties, especially from my point of view, to let all those other Number One Wives know I was a Number One Wife too. Oh my goodness, that meant acting with decorum and never letting the side down — what a tall order that turned out to be!

Working Girl!

Wonders will never cease, from being a bit of a lost soul I was now a working girl! Golly gosh. I had been at this lark for a couple of weeks and hadn't been rumbled yet, and by using all my amazing skills had managed to sort of tame the typewriter. By this I mean I had actually executed a perfect letter in just under an hour. In fact, I had exceeded and maybe surpassed my own expectations!

I think actions speak louder than words, so this surely must have been a sign of progress. Something told me that Mr IBM and I might just have forged an understanding and could finally become working companions. I hesitated to shout this too loudly, but fingers crossed.

I now felt confident enough not to panic too much every time he took off on his own, whereas before I felt I needed to don my running shoes just to keep up. Now I just sat languidly waiting for him to stop teasing me, I know he thought he had the upper hand but maybe, just maybe, I might have been catching up. I had awarded myself seven out of ten for this remarkable progress, but between you and me it had been against all odds.

How on earth I found myself masquerading as a secretary in this dismal back office in Dubai I will never know. My secret had to be by using lashings of guile and oh so sweet a smile, although this was not the time to bask in reflected glory or become complacent because I needed to stay on top of my game if I wasn't to be booted out. Actually, it was like being a character in some crazy sitcom when you had the definite feeling that possibly you had been miscast but had to keep up the pretence, not unlike a game of charades.

Sitting quietly one day minding my own business I was to discover something that would surely take my breath away. What was this astonishing information? Well, in those days Dubai was known for importing gigantic quantities of non-ferrous metals into the country but, once landed, what happened to this cargo? Well, I will tell you where some of it went and how this was happening right under my little nose.

One day the boss came in and said, 'Drop everything and come with me, Jan'. I followed as he proceeded to dash past the Indian clerks who, with heads down, were still diligently adding up goodness knows what on their calculators. We rushed out of the main door, across the corridor and into the main office, which was, in fact, an apartment identical to ours but two floors below.

He careered past a beautiful sultry lady, sitting behind a desk which seemed to be covered in ticker tape that was engulfing her as well. Beside her was a giant telex machine which was spewing out tape as if its life depended on it. I was to discover that these were the up-to-the minute gold and silver prices being quoted by all the major commodity markets from around the world, which this beautiful lady, with no name, was logging into a giant ledger. My God, what was going on?

Surely this was a total den of iniquity. There was no time to tarry though, as we dashed passed and breathlessly landing up on the balcony. 'Look,' said the boss. All I could see were dhows moored on the quayside, nothing new, but the boss was by then really agitated. He said, 'They are doing a "run" tonight'. What was he talking about? Maybe he had got a touch of the sun!

All was then revealed. There was to be a 'gold run' to the subcontinent that night and six dhows were taking part. It was explained to me that they would sail in convoy, but the wonderment was that although the dhows all outwardly looked the same, two of them were fitted with twin-screw propellers. This was to enable the convoy to outwit the local coastguards once they were sailing inside territorial waters, as they would without a doubt have been spotted.

The plan was that the two dhows in question would break loose from the convoy and head for a predestined point at breakneck speed, whilst the other dhows would act as decoys. The gold would be offloaded and once all transactions were complete they would sail into the sunset with happy crews who, more to the point, were now richer than when they set off. Their hearts might have been beating rather rapidly though!

Gosh, what excitement, this was the stuff of the Boy's Own Paper, especially as at that time it was forbidden to hold gold bullion in the UK. Consequently, this made the whole operation appear clandestine, risqué and romantic in equal measure, and to think I was privy to such goings on. They were scheduled to depart that evening and consequently I was able to watch from the safety of 'our balcony'. Naturally the big fear was that six would leave but maybe fewer would return, but that was the risk the crews took — no risk no gain, as they say.

Now I knew why there were always so many ragtags patiently queuing to enter the 'front office'. I was to discover that they were the locals wagering their small offerings for large returns, not unlike having a punt on the Grand National, and optimism had to be the name of the game.

There was one very curious omission though. When handing over their bounty, the amount was registered by the lady with no name, together with their identity, in a giant ledger, but no receipts were ever issued!

Until the dhows returned there was a palpable tension in the air and, naturally, there was a collective sigh of relief when the convoy was sighted sailing up the Creek and noted to be miraculously intact. There were then smiling faces all around and the tension that had hung over the Souk for days quietly evaporated — mission accomplished!

Before you ask, no I never succumbed. I was too awestruck at what was going on right under my little nose! Actually, at that time, I was relishing being the proud owner of my first 22 carat gold necklace. I reckoned I had earned it — don't you?

Bizarre Twist!

Oh, what a mad few days that had been. There seemed to be a little bit of excitement around every corner and now I was really swooning at the thought that I had a little secret, which is that there were gold smugglers in my midst; oh, what next!

It was extraordinary that after only a few months away from that green and pleasant land that I did, or is it still do, call home my days had taken on a very bizarre twist. Although I hadn't wagered my last shilling on the outcome of the dhows' overseas expedition event I was waiting with baited breath to learn whether the convoy had arrived back intact!

Looking over the balcony early one morning, there they all were tucked up safe and sound having quietly sailed up the Creek under the cover of darkness. Now, if that wasn't enough proof, the jungle drums had obviously been beating down the Souk heralding their arrival, because the ragtags were already lining up for their payout — happiness all around, I would say!

So with that little excitement over I was now to be found each morning whiling away the time in my little back office, more often than not sitting quietly recovering from the night before, and the boss was normally doing the same! Oh, what havoc the Dubai nightlife was causing one and all.

Talking about nightlife, I had just been told that there was a swish nightclub in the square behind the apartments, which was called the Sahara. Its existence would have been difficult to detect in daylight because it was situated on the first floor of an extremely nondescript building, and it was only at night when the lights were on above the door that one had any idea that this building may hold a secret or two.

Actually, on reflection it could only be in Dubai that the most sought after address in town, for a night out, was reached across a pile of sand. Initially, that was not a very promising start to a night of reveries, and definitely not good for one's dancing pumps either, but once inside all one's misgivings evaporated as we were instantly whisked into another world, as if by magic.

It was with great excitement and anticipation that we accepted an invitation to join a jolly party one Thursday evening, and it sure didn't disappoint. The invitation was all the more intriguing because we had no idea as to what to expect on reaching the top of those stairs that very first visit, maybe a little like climbing the stairway to heaven.

It transpired that the Sahara was owned and run by Lebanese businessmen. The club was intimate with banquettes covered in red velvet; there was gold filigree everywhere together with ornate lighting, which created an extremely sophisticated aura.

Considering its location, to say being introduced to this little gem was an amazement would be a complete understatement; its existence was quite phenomenal. Then one's eyes were drawn to the end of this little room where, wonder of wonders, there was a dance floor and, oh, a band. I was captivated.

Once inside one could never have imagined for a moment that this gem of a place was sitting in the middle of dusty Dubai. We were immediately transported into another world, a world of make-believe perhaps, nevertheless one full of fun and laughter. We piled onto the banquettes, ordered drinks and merrily danced the night away.

There were a few little problems though. One was that the band was so loud your eardrums were blown to pieces and the other was that there weren't enough girls to go round! Good for the girls but on occasions the husbands became somewhat miffed at the lack of attention they were being shown by their darling wives!

The owners had managed to create an atmosphere that would have been commonplace in Beirut with great aplomb and naturally we loved the entire experience because, even in London, there would have been few places that could have matched this little 'gem' for style.

On reflection, it was way ahead of its time especially in downtown Dubai and we all adored it. Mohammed, the maître d', was a firm favourite with us girls, always looking suave in his dinner jacket and overseeing proceedings with quiet efficiency.

It really was quite extraordinary how contradictory Dubai was, as outwardly it offered so little. Without the Creek running through its veins it would have been utterly nondescript and yet there was a quiet mystery about the place that was captivating. Not realizing that it is happening one slowly falls in love with the place, which is so hard to comprehend as it seems to happen so unexpectedly; it just creeps up from behind and from there on in one is hooked.

It's the early morning sunrises over the Creek and beyond into the desert; it's the mullahs calling the faithful to prayer. It's the dhows jostling for space to moor; it's the 'phut phut' of the abras crossing the Creek from Deira to Dubai, transporting passengers from one side to the other, who are going about their business.

Then it's the sun setting out to sea over the Persian Gulf, a sight money just can't buy, which is the signal for the Souk to come alive with the sounds and smells of the evening before once again the faithful are called to prayer, which heralds the end of another memorable day, Dubai style.

Yes, I was totally bewitched!

A *Little Affronted!*

Just when I was thinking that we had 'cracked it' – that is to say we had managed to establish a daily routine that was running almost like clockwork – yes, you have guessed it, it was all too good to be true. It's what one gets by becoming a little too complacent.

What had happened now? Well, I will tell you. I usually returned from my stint of propping up the typewriter at around noon, which was not an overtaxing stint in the office, four hours to be precise! I then had to while away the time somehow until Mike's return a couple of hours later when we usually had lunch.

Whatever I found to do was normally accompanied by a cooling lager. It must be remembered that I had by now relinquished all household responsibilities including cooking — a lady of leisure was I. Oh, the joy, I reckoned if I managed to play my cards right I would never, ever have to pick up a duster in anger again, not a bad achievement at the tender age of 28!

This particular lunchtime Mike remarked that I seemed to be consuming rather a lot of lagers before his return. That day he reckoned twelve cans and pointed out that it really was not the 'done' thing, actually not lady like at all. This was surely a wrap on the knuckles. Needless to say I was more than a little affronted, but it was definitely true the beers were, in fact, disappearing at a rate of knots, but how and where to?

All was soon revealed when an Egyptian neighbour collared Mike one day to say he was seeing extraordinary goings on outside our front door on a daily basis. What was he about to divulge? Well, it transpired that our Ali was seen most days furtively sneaking across the corridor clutching packages which he deposited in the meter cupboard, obviously thinking he was invisible.

On inspection, the packages contained a few cans of lager and usually a small amount of decanted Scotch. At least I was exonerated but poor old Ali was most definitely for the high jump. The consensus of opinion was that he had to go. Consequently, the good ship Constable was thrown totally off course; in fact, it had sailed into a veritable whirlwind. Why? Because the captain of all things domestic hadn't a clue as to where to start.

Consequently, the most pressing problem was how we were going to be able to find a suitable replacement before we sank without trace under a pile of dirty laundry. The word was duly put about that Apartment 603 needed rescuing rapidly from an impending major disaster.

They say worse things happen at sea but at that particular moment in time I could not think of anything worse than having to fill the bath up with hot soapy water, fling in our dirty washing and then get in myself and trample all over it — in other words, turn myself into a 'Hotpoint'. But as they say, when in Rome!

We were now slowly beginning to appreciate what was happening in Dubai. Outwardly it was just a track of desert bordering the Persian Gulf with apparently not a lot to offer either man or beast. But if one scratched the surface a little, a veritable story book of amazing tales came tumbling out of just how the development of Dubai was being envisaged, and the visionary was one man, Sheikh Rashid, the amazing ruler of Dubai.

Sheikh Rashid was a man of the desert but he was bright enough to realize that if Dubai was not furnished with the wherewithal to enable it to start making its presence felt as an international trader then it would be unable to make much progress.

In 1967, Phase One of Port Rashid was commissioned, which initially had four berths and was scheduled for completion in 1972.

Dubai was, and always had been, a trading post with goods entering and leaving on a daily basis, either by dhow or merchant ship, the latter having to moor offshore as there were no deep water berths. Consequently, the building of a port was indeed a necessity, as was the airport. A new airport was in the throes of being built when we arrived in 1970, which was scheduled for completion in early 1971.

Once these two facilities were fully commissioned it would effectively be saying to the outside world, 'Hi there, here we are up and running and ready for business, and given a little time we may give you a run for your money!' There is many a true word spoken in jest.

Both these projects were being overseen by British companies, hence the plethora of young British engineers in our midst who worked hard and played hard and were always ready for a party, where swinging from the chandeliers was usually par for the course.

These new facilities naturally required road access and, to this end, Mike's Bitumen Supply Company was commissioned to provide the asphalt to rectify this matter, which enabled a single lane road to be built between Dubai and Abu Dhabi together with many internal roads. These initial projects were the foundations on which today's Dubai has risen quite spectacularly and in a comparatively short space of time.

There was still one thing missing and that was a golf course and club. Evidentially there had been a nine-hole sand course along the creek, somewhat before our time, which had ceased to exist much to the chagrin of the 'boys'.

Help was at hand though, as Shcik Rashid kindly ceded a piece of desert to help to rectify this matter. This piece of land, actually desert, was out on the Alweer Road, which was somewhat difficult to reach but nevertheless an enormous breakthrough for all budding expat golfers!

What a challenge it proved to be to transform those sand dunes into something resembling a golf course, which eventually became the pride and joy of every golfer in Dubai.

How that was achieved is another story!

Golf course, Dubai Country Club

Barking Mad!

I had heard of making a silk purse out of a sow's ear but never of creating a golf course out of a track of sand with not a blade of grass in sight. This surely should be a sight to behold once completed and, quite naturally, utterly unique.

It just goes to show what fanatics golfers are and what lengths they will go to in order to be able to pursue their beloved sport. Or maybe, just maybe they are all barking mad. In this case, only time would tell!

Mike volunteered, or was he commandeered, to join the working party. Being a keen golfer, he was only too eager to help, along with many others. Many a glass of 'hooch' was consumed whilst deciding how this job was to be tackled as obviously I don't think any of the working parties had had much previous experience in this field.

Creating a golf course out of a track of sand must come top of the list of one of the most bizarre challenges presented to man. Consequently, it became much easier to envisage this wondrous course miraculously rising out of this unpromising terrain and then daydreaming about hosting amazing championships after a few glasses too many, or I should say 'one over the eight'.

Without Johnnie Walker's assistance, I'm not sure whether the project would have ever got off the ground. At least he came from the home of golf, bonny Scotland, so consequently had to be a good talisman.

Where there's a will there's a way. Nobody in their right minds would have headed into the desert in search of this 'gift' of land from Sheik Rashid because it sure wasn't a feather-bedded journey.

The first part of this trek took one inland along a tarmac road, which had been purposely built to enable enormous lorries to reach an inland quarry in double-quick time. These lorries were on a mission collecting rocks necessary to fashion the new port. Sharing a road with these thunderous vehicles was quite terrifying as their drivers seemed hell-bent on self-destruction and also the destruction of anything in their path.

It was with enormous relief when one turned off this stretch of road; at least then one's blood pressure subsided and one's heart retreated to its normal place. The next stage was bumping along a subka track whilst looking for a mound of sand with a tree perched on top. On seeing this, you took a right and prayed that the car would not become bogged down in the sand as you manoeuvred your way onwards and upwards, and on reaching the tree you knew you had made it.

Actually, once there it looked a little like the surface of the moon and I am quite sure the moon might just have been a little easier to get to! This track of land was at the head of the Creek and in the hazy distance one could just make out downtown Deira and the Al Maktoum Bridge, but looking inland there was desert as far as the eye could see with very little vegetation and only an occasional camel for company.

The plan was to find a suitable mound or hillock, call it what you will, for the first tee, mark the spot and then pace the necessary distance to where the green would be. Now that was too funny for words as the greens just metamorphosed into browns.

These browns were achieved by pouring oil on the sand, then rolling it to create a flat putting surface, and then a stake would be placed as a marker for the hole. I am sure you will realize that to be part of this venerable 'team' you needed a very fertile imagination!

This process was repeated another eight times and after much too-ing and fro-ing, and I'm sure cussing and blinding, the nine-hole course at the Country Club came into being. The camels enjoyed this activity enormously and would usually, once left on their own overnight, play wonderful games that involved pulling up the stakes, thinking they were mini trees and that they had been put there just for them.

By this time, the original scouting party needed assistance and the 'boys' from the port were press-ganged into helping with the fashioning of the 'browns', which they did with great efficiency. I wonder just how many people have spent an enjoyable afternoon pottering around that desert course over the ensuing years — my guess is many, many thousands. What a team effort and what a legacy.

Before the inaugural shot could be fired, as it were, there was another conundrum which had to be tackled. How could a reasonably perfect lie be achieved? Teeing off was not a problem but once on the 'fairway' what did one do? All manner of golfing etiquette books were consulted and I'm quite sure somebody would have had a quiet word with the Royal and Ancient, but eventually this little problem was resolved.

Initially, preferred lies were the obvious solution — to the uninitiated, a preferred lie is where one is able to move the ball to make it easier to play the shot. I am not too sure but I think this was not to be more than a club's length from where the ball had landed, but not closer to the hole.

As time went by a better solution was discovered and that was to carry a piece of AstroTurf whilst playing. Once the ball had been located, the turf was positioned alongside it, the ball was then placed onto the turf and played from that position. The turf was only required for the fairways as putting was not a problem; this was because the 'browns' played quite true.

The other sticking point was that the usual white ball would be very difficult to locate in the sand, so it was agreed to substitute with red balls instead. The ingenuity of these golf mad chaps knew no bounds. Once these minor details were in place, the game was ready to commence.

The tenacity and bulldog spirit displayed by these golfing fanatics who oversaw this amazing achievement should not be underestimated. This is the story of the birth of Dubai Country Club where many a happy hour was subsequently spent, pitching and putting one's wits against the elements, the heat – yes, it was oh so hot – one's opponent, oneself and, not least, the oh so crazy course.

Last and by no means least were the camels that sauntered past, and maybe stopped and stared, and possibly thought to themselves, 'I always knew men were crazy but this is ridiculous and they are not even equipped with two humps to enable them to withstand the searing heat. The sun has obviously gone to their heads!'

Once again that ditty penned by Noel Coward, which is so apt, springs to mind, 'Mad dogs and Englishmen go out in the midday sun'!

Special Offer!

I had just heard that BOAC were running 'special offers' on travel from London to Dubai; I wonder why? Maybe, just maybe, nobody wanted, or had any particular reason, to visit this hot and dusty little speck on the globe.

I had a surprise for BOAC though because I knew of two people who would more than jump at the chance of revisiting the Persian Gulf. It would sure bring a smile to their faces to receive a very unexpected opportunity to wander down their very special memory lane — a trip they would never have envisaged being able to make before their daughter, yes that's me, landed up in Dubai.

Actually, once the subject was broached they couldn't get there quickly enough. I must explain that my father was a research chemist and in 1929, on leaving university, he joined the Anglo Iranian Oil Company, as BP was called then, and little did he know what lay before him. He was posted to Abadan in Persia, a heady prospect, and a posting most definitely not for the faint-hearted.

The journey took three weeks from leaving Victoria Station in London to arriving in Abadan, which was quite daunting as in those days most of the travelling was either by ship, overland or even Shanks's pony.

By comparison, arriving in Dubai after enjoying a luxurious flight on a VC10 would be a total doddle. I broached the subject and, as it was November and coming up for Christmas, what better present could we offer them. As expected, they were as ecstatic as I was because although I had embraced my new life I was still a little homesick and was sure their visit would sort me out! That turned out to be the understatement of the year!

I was counting the days until their arrival and I'm sure they were doing the same. They were scheduled to hit town ten days before Christmas and stay well into January. As this was our first 'Dubai' Christmas we were not too sure what to expect. Dubai didn't disappoint because, as it turned out, the order of the day was party after party after party, naturally with Naomi and Gordon in toe. Would you have expected anything else?

The day of their arrival was duly upon us and the excitement was palpable. Naturally, the whole of Dubai knew of their coming and that included British Petroleum, my father's alma mater. It transpired that as far as anybody was aware in the entire existence of BP in the Gulf, nobody had heard of a BP pensioner visiting, especially to take a holiday! Maybe bidding a hasty retreat was more the norm!

The BP boat was definitely going to be pushed out to mark this momentous occasion. There was great excitement and great expectations all round! So we had not given too much thought that company protocol was about to be turned on its head, which on reflection was a little naive. We were only too delighted that my parents were obviously in for a much unexpected experience of a lifetime, or rather another experience of a lifetime!

I must now explain. What we hadn't given any thought to whatsoever, or more importantly I hadn't, was the fact that Mike worked for Shell International Petroleum. In those days, BP and Shell were arch rivals in the Gulf, even though Mike had been seconded to set up a joint BP/Shell company. Old habits die hard and, consequently, on occasions Mike found himself the proverbial piggy in the middle, and at times that was not an enviable position to find oneself in.

Everything changed once the VC10 had taxied to a standstill, the steps had been positioned and the doors opened because there were my parents, poised at the top of the steps and ready to take Dubai by storm. Yes, it's true, once one has lived in the Gulf a little piece stays with one forever. This was borne out by the look of sheer wonderment and excitement on their faces at the prospect of renewing their acquaintance, firstly, I think, with the Gulf and secondly with little old me!

I was too excited for words with the wonderment of it all and this time there were no tears just smiles of sheer joy and happiness. I knew that Naomi and Gordon would be eager to immerse themselves with the sights, sounds and smells of Arabia once again and, naturally, I was eager to show them our new home, Dubai. This was surely going to be a very emotional trip down memory lane.

They had imagined our life would be like the one they had left behind all those years ago, a real hardship posting. Instead, they found Dubai most agreeable and very civilized, and I think they might have liked to stay forever — now that's what one calls progress!

In their day, there was no air conditioning, only punka-wallers. These were boys who would sit on the floor manually operating fans by a string attached to their big toes, which afforded a little light relief from the searing heat. As it was so hot, they had to sleep on the flat roof of the bungalow in order to take advantage of any vestige of breeze that might flutter their way.

They would possibly have climbed into the refrigerator, if they had had one! In those days, an 'iceman' used to arrive at the bungalow each morning with blocks of ice, this being the substitute for a mechanical refrigerator — it was almost like the Stone Age! This did not deter them from rising to the challenge and embracing the life that was on offer with gusto and, by the looks on their faces in Dubai, they were about to do it once again.

I thought I would be guiding them around and would hear them saying, 'Well done, darling, you have settled down well under very trying circumstances,' but all I was regaled with was, 'this place is truly wonderful', 'you are so lucky to be here', 'it beats visiting you in Surrey, hands down!' and questions of when they would be off to the Souk, the swimming pool, partying, sightseeing and anything else we or they could think of — I feel giddy just thinking about it now!

Then – would you believe it – my mother came up with the bright idea that an audience with Sheik Rashid would surely be the icing on the cake and would round off her trip nicely, notwithstanding the fact that women didn't really figure in Arabian society.

Yes, I then had a fainting fit and a sense of humour failure all rolled into one, which was not a nice sensation. What had we let ourselves in for? What was I to do? And, if all her bright ideas came off, would Mike lose his job and, even worse, would we be beheaded?

Matters became even worse once they had been let loose on Dubai society because they were really far more experienced at this expat lark than the majority of the people they were meeting. The stories they had to recount were quite remarkable compared to ours in 1970 and, more to the point, they had lived to tell them with a smile on their faces, in spite of all the hazards and hardships they had had to endure. My father had actually contracted smallpox while in Abadan and was obviously not expected to survive. He was quarantined way out in the desert beside a lake, with a bearer to attend to his needs, but miraculously survived.

By the time they had met up with the BP personnel there was no stopping them, and what a marvellous reception they were given. Then to crown it all I was christened the 'BP baby' by the General Manager of BP, when really I was a 'Shell wife'; whatever was going to happen to me? The Empty Quarter here I come!

Epic Visit!

All I wanted to know is if we would live to tell the tale. What tale? The tale of a pair of BP pensioners who, unaided, had managed to take Dubai by storm and flatten us into the bargain.

We were coming to the end of Naomi's and Gordon's epic visit and were not too sure, at present, if we would ever make it to the last furlong. Instead of Christmas parties it was now farewell parties, held especially for them, and they sure were going out with a bang. At least my mother had not found a way of organizing an audience with Sheik Rashid before her departure but she had definitely laid down the gauntlet for her next visit, which was pencilled in for eleven months hence! It would take that long for us to recover. What a to-do!

I can now say with utter certainty that once we had dispatched them, I realized that it was their visit that I must have been subconsciously waiting for, as it put everything into perspective. After that, I never looked back and I too began taking Dubai by storm! The love affair had truly begun, which I can honestly say has lasted to this day, a mere 43 years and is still going strong.

What does that say about that strip of desert straddled by the Persian Gulf? I think, perhaps, it must say that it possessed unseen magical qualities that weaved a spell and scattered a little stardust too because, almost without exception, we all seemed to succumb to its charm and fall madly in love with it.

Not bad going, that was two batterings I had had in the space of nine months; the first arriving in Dubai and the second surviving this whirlwind visit. We settled back into our old routine but now with more gusto, seeing our new way of life from a totally different perspective. Dare I say it, it looked quite good too!

The apartment never seemed to be empty as quietly we had been adopted by the 'boys' from BOAC who were flying freighters from London to Hong Kong via Dubai, where they normally stopped over for a couple of nights.

The majority of these pilots lived near or around Camberley from whence we came, and a bartering arrangement was soon established. We provided the Heinekens and, in return, they got their wives to buy up half of Marks and Spencer for me, to be delivered on their next trip. My imagination didn't stop there and soon I was ordering from Hong Kong too. This little lark must have been the forerunner of Internet shopping — my, I was ahead of the times! Never let an opportunity pass you by, that's what I say!

The apartment was also becoming the 'home from home' for the Sharjah boys; these were the super military chaps along with the BOAC crews who had taken pity on us whilst we were in the hotel. They nearly always visited Dubai when they knew a plane from London was due, as they wanted to be first to greet the hostesses who would be on board, such gallant gentlemen! Actually, their very unsubtle manoeuvres always amused us and brought a smile to our faces.

By way of reciprocation, we enjoyed dinners at the Officers' Mess followed by the latest film. These dinners were always grand affairs with no shortage of ingredients for the chefs as all their food was flown in. Naturally, we loved these invitations.

Again, it was another surreal experience because to get there one had to drive to Sharjah, and I think in those early days it was just a subka road, or maybe a single lane tarmac job – you will get the drift, it was nothing splendiferous – and then one sort of took a right and ventured into the desert. Before one's eyes was an official barrier announcing that you had arrived at RAF Sharjah, which was usually manned by local chaps who were normally praying – so much for security – and the barrier was usually raised! Nothing new there!

They also introduced us to Sheik Robin, a jeweller in the Sharjah Souk, who was frequented by most of the military personnel; he was affectionately nicknamed Robin Bastard! What an experience that was; he used to sit cross-legged fashioning fine pieces of gold or silver with the most basic of tools using methods that would have hardly changed since biblical times.

He was obviously very astute and knew how to play the 'boys' at their own game or should I say play along with them, as they used to rib him unmercifully. He was taught many swear words into the bargain, and I suspect he had no idea of the meaning of any of them.

For their trouble, I expect the boys were more than slightly overcharged, that being his sweet justice, but nobody really cared. It did not take long for me to fall under his spell either and I soon placed my first order with him for a gold rope necklace — now that was a real red-letter day.

We were fast approaching the end of our first year and were being advised by all the old Kahais from East Africa that, instead of going straight back to the UK, we should take the opportunity of visiting that wonderful country before it was ruined. Who would have imagined that we would have had such a choice, but these were the spoils of war! So plans were duly made and the jungle drums started beating, heralding our impending arrival, as in those days visitors were introduced long arm and, on arrival, scooped up and wined and dined with warmth and generosity.

Then a terrible catastrophe occurred. Dubai was hit by a cholera scare, which was truly very scary indeed. The authorities were quick to take action, which actually meant that for the ensuing few months all imports of fresh produce were banned. This was chaos for us, as Dubai did not produce any edibles at all. We survived with difficulty, although it was tough going and very frightening.

Again we had a piece of luck, because at that time P&O ships used to dock in Dubai occasionally and if one was lucky enough to know the agent and, more importantly, he liked the cut of your jib, you were invited on board for dinner, which was actually a right royal feast. These feasts were so stupendous that they were enough to keep one going until another invitation came one's way to the Officers' Mess in Sharjah.

We managed to survive with guile and a little help from our new found friends. And, I think, by taking a leaf out of the book of those other beasts of the desert, my friends, the camels, who were so adept at keeping body and soul together under the most trying of circumstances. Thank goodness though that we didn't start developing a couple of humps.

The day was fast approaching for our lift-off to Nairobi, so it was time for a little reflection. We were leaving having achieved what we thought was a miracle. Twelve months earlier we were making our way to an altogether different airport full of heartache, anguish and uncertainty as to what lay before us, and now we were heading to a very different airport with a spring in our step, a smile on our faces and a home to return to.

Also, to make life all the sweeter I had been offered an amazing job by BOAC to be their first ground hostess, working during the mornings, at the newly opened Dubai International Airport when I returned. My goodness, what a difference a year can make!

Jumping for Joy!

We were jumping for joy. We were fast approaching the end of our first year and would shortly be heading off for two months' leave. I am not sure how happiness is defined in the Oxford Dictionary but anybody looking at us would have had little doubt that we were happiness personified!

We had survived this tortuous year with a smile on our faces, two feet on the ground, money in the bank and would shortly be embarking on another adventure, but this time one of our own volition. Yes, we were heading off to East Africa to say 'hello' to all those lions and tigers that lived there and maybe get to stroke an elephant! Unimaginable twelve months ago. Nairobi here we come!

We were off, our first port of call being Dubai Airport for the Air India flight to Bombay along with lots of excited Indian families who would shortly be reunited with their families. There was a great sense of excitement; we were embarking on an adventure, but they were all heading home.

Everybody was wearing their Sunday best, and there was a flurry of new silken saris and gentlemen looking very dapper, sporting beards and moustaches. These were suitably trimmed with the whole ensemble being topped off, in some instances, by magnificent turbans. Dare I say it, there was also a slight whiff of curry in the air; total exotica.

The flight to Bombay was relatively short and before we knew it we had landed and found ourselves in another world completely. At first sight it sure looked like utter chaos, but possibly organized chaos; we would never really know as it took us a while to reorientate. Finding ourselves, our bags and a taxi to take us downtown to the magnificently named Taj Hotel was a major achievement.

'Hey, we are seasoned expats now so nothing is meant to faze us,' we said stoically, that was until the taxi headed downtown. The roads were totally jammed with old cars, rickshaws and poor, poor people all vying for the little space that was vacant. We seemed to be jammed right in the middle of this quite astonishing mass.

As we slowly inched our way forward, we realized that the people we saw were actually camping along the roadside adjacent to a drainage ditch that housed the most repugnant stagnant water. This was their home where all their daily functions were performed. Many were hatched, matched and dispatched there, never knowing any other way of life — we were shaken to the core realizing how incredible lucky we were.

We eventually arrived outside the Taj, as it was affectionately called, somewhat chastened; but, on entering, were immediately catapulted into a breathtaking world of grace, splendour and beauty. Bombay was definitely a city of two halves. We were ushered into the foyer by a liveried doorman, which was breathtaking in its opulence. Our first impressions were of an enormous space which exuded peace and tranquillity.

This aura was created by the most amazing black and white marbled floor and the most glorious domed glass ceiling which allowed shafts of golden sunlight to dance through. These shafts alighted hither and yon, on the wonderful colourful saris being worn by those ladies that lunch and also on the copious amounts of glorious tropical plants, which were everywhere. Had we entered paradise, I wondered!

Having checked-in, we were ushered to our room which was reached along an open corridor, from which we were able to look down onto the foyer. It was as if an amazing theatrical production was taking place before our eyes, as the foyer was alive, being seduced by the music being played by the palm court orchestra. The only tune that could have adequately summed up this tableau was 'I Could Have Danced

All Night', and all day too for that matter, from My Fair Lady. What a magnificent spectacle, totally splendiferous — I'm sure even the plants were swaying in time to the music. Oh, my goodness.

We explored. The foyer opened out onto a beautiful tropical garden where a manicured lawn took centre stage with a supporting cast of tropical plants and flowers, making it a haven for the exotic birds that were flying in and out singing their happy tunes. To complete the picture, along the outer walls of the hotel was an open conservatory where tables were laid for refreshments and flunkeys were poised to see to one's every wish; yes, I was absolutely certain that this must be paradise.

We were ushered to a vacant table which was exquisitely set for afternoon tea; yes, English afternoon tea. This was served with warm scones, home-made jam, Victoria sponge and, to complete this amazing spectacle, a pot of Indian tea together with milk and sugar, all served by waiters, resplendent in their white uniforms.

All the tables were taken up by beautiful people — Indian ladies resplendent in their colourful attire, some being accompanied by their husbands, who cut quite a dash, but mostly they were taking tea with their lady friends and no doubt having a little gossip.

Then there were the formidable memsahibs, some also being accompanied by their husbands who were wearing tropical whites and sporting the obligatory enormous bushy moustaches; they were oh so different from the suave Indian gentlemen.

The memsahibs were, in the main, wearing typical English afternoon tea dresses and some were even carrying little white gloves. Many were looking a little careworn, possibly wishing that they were taking tea far, far away in an English country garden, which in the height of summer would have been perfumed by the scent of roses together with amazing cottage garden blooms; an oasis of tranquillity.

Yes, it was another world and for many where they would have been happier if, like me, fate hadn't played a hand. There was only thing missing to complete this quintessentially English picture and that was the sound of leather on willow and a plummy voice shouting 'six not out'!

What am I doing here, I thought. Ah yes, we had survived our first year in Dubai and this was the beginning of our great escape. Well, it sure was different, with not a speck of sand to be seen. I had forgotten that a beautiful garden is a sight to behold, and the gardens at the Taj were just that. It was like taking a walk on the other side of heaven.

All too soon our stay came to an end but we could not depart before we had walked over to take a look at and pay homage to the famous monument, the Gateway to India, which was a short walk from the hotel.

This famous monument was built to commemorate the visit of King George V and Queen Mary to India in 1924, after which it later became the ceremonial entrance to India for viceroys and overlooks the Arabian Sea. For many a first timer it must have been a stomach wrenching moment knowing that on its sighting it could be the start of an adventure of a lifetime and for others a life sentence. Oh, what a lottery, sometimes life was so unfair and dealt the most terrible hands to those least able to cope.

We hadn't realized that whilst inside the hotel we were cocooned in a world of privilege and luxury but, once outside, the stark reality was that most of the population of Bombay were not in that category. To reach the monument we literally had to step over, around and through the most underprivileged people we had ever seen, or could imagine existed, on this planet.

Yes, once again we witnessed whole families camping out on the pavement, a little piece of the world they called home, but this time we were walking amongst them. I am sure that when this magnificent monument was being built, the powers that be never envisaged it would become a refuge for the homeless along with the Bombay pigeons and crows; at least the birds had the ability to spread their wings and fly away.

To our shame we scuttled back to the hotel rather smartly, feeling somewhat chastened. After that harrowing excursion we were in need of a stiff drink but, in those days, there was prohibition in India so we had to settle for stiff lemonade.

We were soon on our way to the airport, this time heading for Nairobi, taking with us amazing memories of our fleeting visit, both happy and sad. Our seat belts were fastened and we were off on the next part of our adventure.

Happy Holidays!

Up, up and away and that was just our blood pressure! By gosh we had done it; yes, we were actually gliding through the stratosphere heading for Nairobi and couldn't begin to imagine what adventures lay in store for us.

The thought of meeting all those wild animals and, perhaps, getting close up and personal was simply unimaginable. I wondered what our reaction would be — only time would tell!

Again, the flying time from Bombay was quite short and we were soon touching down in East Africa, as it was called in those heady, slightly decadent days. Yes, we were ready, willing and more than able to take on and enjoy whatever this country had to offer. The atmosphere at Nairobi Airport was very different from Bombay, as it was somewhat cooler and far less frenetic. Our first impression was that the Africans were a little more laid-back than the Indians.

We were soon heading downtown to the famous Norfolk Hotel. I wondered how it would compare to the Taj in style and opulence. Were we becoming like two little upstarts, possibly a couple of little Lord Fauntleroys, in such a short space of time? Because that would never do!

Actually, we arrived at night and found the Norfolk to be a single-storey building with, I think, a thatched roof, being long, low and understated. As it was dark, we could not take in our surroundings and, consequently, everything had to be put on hold until the morning.

Morning dawned with a new day and a new continent. Yes, this time we really were brimming with anticipation having heard endless stories about this wonderful country, and reckoned it was now our turn to sample all the delights it had to offer. We even had the gear, including pith helmets! We must outwit those animals somehow!

Our first port of call was to the restaurant for breakfast. Well we were awestruck, as before us was a table as long as forever, groaning with such an abundance of fruits the likes of which we had never seen, let alone sampled. This encounter was especially amazing as we had so recently come from Dubai with its ban on the import of fresh produce.

We were dizzy with anticipation and desperate to savour these delights. Which fruit should we sample first and could I really eat a whole pineapple? Actually, neither of us realized that there were so many different types of fruit growing in the whole wide world; what an amazement, and what a sight for sore eyes. We made a beeline for the table, piling our plates high with a little piece of this and a little piece of that — far, far too much but what the hell.

As we were tucking into this delicious array of fruit, a wonderful plate of freshly cooked bacon and eggs, sunny side up of course, was placed before us. Oh the joy, we were in foodie breakfast heaven! We were marvelling at our luck, not only to have found ourselves in East Africa but to have stumbled upon this wonderful breakfast, enjoying every mouthful as if it was to be our last. Golly gosh, what fun this was turning out to be. Do you think we can have a breakfast like this every day, we asked ourselves. If so, we will never want to leave!

We then heard the tinkling of a bell, which heralded the arrival of the bellboy who was carrying an enormous placard. The sound of the ringing bell was to attract the diners' attention, as it did ours. Imagine our surprise when we saw 'Constable', our name, written on the board. We nearly choked on our bacon. Who knew we were there? Well we were about to discover.

Behind the boy walked a very imposing lady. Introductions were made and she explained that she had been detailed by her East African chums, who now lived in Dubai, to look out for us, and so she was doing just that. We had only been on terra firma for approximately twelve hours and already we were being scooped up, and an itinerary was being outlined; it was so kind. My, what a difference a day makes.

Yesterday we were being reminded of the injustices that exist in this world, seeing all those poor people in India who were simply unable to help themselves to better their lot. Now, with breathtaking speed, we had been transported into another world, which at first glance appeared to be full of privileges and where everyone had a smile on their faces, or was it that we were seeing our first day in East Africa through rose coloured spectacles — jambo!

A song springs to mind, 'Oh, what a beautiful morning, oh, what a beautiful day, the corn is as high as an elephant's eye and everything is going my way'. I'd soon be off to see a real live elephant; how amazing was that? I wondered if she was called Nellie.

Phyllida kindly escorted us to our car, introduced us to the driver, and then we were off, with the first port of call being the Nairobi Central Fruit and Vegetable Market. I just loved markets and this certainly didn't disappoint. It was awesome; yes, a sight to behold. The fresh flowers were stacked as high as an elephant's eye, and I was completely overwhelmed at the different varieties.

Yes, many were familiar, like roses, but then there were so many others that were indigenous to Africa. It was a dazzling kaleidoscope of colours on which to feast one's eyes and, together with the wonderful perfume, it made one go weak at the knees. No wonder, because the only flowers I had seen since leaving England a year ago were plastic ones, and they were truly no substitute for the real thing!

We entered the body of the market and all one could see was an amazing patchwork of colour being made up by a plethora of the freshest fruit and vegetables known to man or woman. My biggest regret was that I could not purchase the lot! But I was presented with the most beautiful bunch of roses by 'my Mike'. It was a superb consolation prize.

We then had a lovely lunch back at the Norfolk with Phyllida and her husband, and learnt a little about life in East Africa for an expat. Oh, it was so different from life in Dubai but I had to remind myself that if Dubai hadn't come our way we wouldn't be in Nairobi now!

We were then escorted by Phyllida for a drive through the Nairobi Game Park; we were surely having too many exciting moments. As we whizzed into the park there was a real live elephant standing there to greet us. Oh my goodness, I am sure he must have known we were coming. I nearly saluted!

We spent the afternoon being driven around this amazing park, which was right in the centre of Nairobi and home to many species of wild animal. It was a taster of what was to come and it was breathtaking. We were like children, wide-eyed in wonderment, especially when we spied yet another variety lolloping through the bushes. Our favourite had to be the elephants – they were so gracious and had such friendly eyes – but, unfortunately, they were a little too large to take home.

After this amazing experience we just had time to return to the Norfolk to bid our farewells and then headed for the railway station to board the night train for Mombasa. Another part of our adventure was about to unfold. The train and route was very famous and we had been assured that we would be following in the footsteps of many an illustrious person. Welcome aboard!

Breathtaking Africa!

My goodness, we had only been on East African soil for a matter of hours, which incidentally was a glorious copper colour, and had eaten our fill of fresh fruit and feasted our eyes on some amazing wild animals, the four-legged variety, I hasten to add! All in all it was a breathtaking experience.

Our whistle-stop tour of Nairobi over, we were now making our way to the Nairobi Railway Station to embark on the famous night train to Mombasa. Another adventure awaited us, and it was so exciting!

As we alighted from our cab, we could feel the excitement in the air, and it reminded me of that song, 'We're all going on a summer holiday'. Mombasa and the Indian Ocean beckoned and that spelled 'summer holiday' to me — what about you?

As we walked along the platform, passed the plush carriages that were painted in brown and cream, the livery of the East African Railways and Harbours Corporation, we heard the whoosh of the steam being exhaled by the engine, which was getting ready to puff us all the way along the track; clickity clack.

We were escorted by a porter who walked us to our designated carriage where we were greeted by our steward who was ready to attend to our every need on this magical journey — this was what travelling in style was all about.

We steamed out of Nairobi and were soon puffing away from the metropolis towards the wide open spaces and our first sighting of the

African bush; a few gazelles were happily frolicking along beside us, trying to keep up with the train. I think they might have done this before!

We were settled into our compartment by our steward, who was smartly attired in the livery of the company. We were served and enjoyed pre-dinner drinks whilst watching the bush unfold before our eyes and marvelling at the beautiful sunset. Yes, this time an African sunset.

After that, we were escorted to the dining car where we enjoyed the most amazing dinner, beautifully served by liveried waiters; those most definitely were the days. Whilst away, our compartment had been made ready for sleeping. It was all so comfortable and all so efficient; this is what we were beginning to get used to in this glorious country. As we were to arrive in Mombasa early in the morning, it was time to sleep and perchance to dream of, guess what, wild animals!

We woke with the larks as the train was still clickity clacking over the rails, chugging us to our destination. Now the sun was rising over the bush and the gazelles were once again dancing to this happy tune, as we gazed in wonder at the amazing scenery scurrying by before our eyes. Naturally, we enjoyed early morning tea whilst enjoying this tableau, which was then followed by a wonderful breakfast and then, low and behold, it was time to disembark.

We alighted from our one-night stand, beguiled and bedazzled but also slightly bemused that one could be so enchanted by an overnight train journey. We then had a little time to stand and stare as we waited to be swept up by our next unsuspecting guide and companion who was going to introduce us to the delights that Mombasa had to offer.

Okay, we were waltzing around East Africa like a couple of swells – yes, those swells who stay at the best hotels – but we were also a little travel naive, never before having had the opportunity of venturing too far from a place called home.

We were beguiled. The station was bathed in the early morning sunlight and was so British in its feel except, obviously, for the gloriously happy, sunny faced Africans who were manning the station, dressed so smartly in the company's livery. There was nothing slipshod about this lot and nothing was too much trouble.

Whilst we were gathering ourselves together and basking in the warmth of the sun, we were hailed by a little lady, who appeared to us to be about a hundred years old. Yes, this was our next guide whilst we were in Mombasa, her parish. Actually, she looked rather frail; boy, were we in for a surprise.

After introductions, she whisked us off to visit Fort Jesus. My goodness, she clambered up hills like a mountain goat, and phew this was a mystery tour, par excellence. We were dashing along after this little lady at a rate of proverbial knots. I'm quite sure we were going to have to make that gin and tonic a treble at this rate!

Our first port of call was Fort Jesus, this being the most famous landmark on Mombasa Island. The fort was originally built by the Portuguese in 1593 on a coral ridge at the entrance to the harbour; this was to ensure the safety of the Portuguese living on the east coast at that time. My goodness, if those walls could speak what tales they would have been able to tell.

After nearly flattening us, our lovely lady graciously invited us to join her for lunch at the famous Mombasa Club, which was housed within the castle walls. Oh my, this was colonial dining at its very best and, yes, we were more than ready for the largest gin and tonic this side of the Equator. Or were pink gins the order of the day? Whatever, we were so happy to be sitting down that as long as there was gin in the glass the colour didn't really matter!

We enjoyed a lovely lunch and were enthralled by the amazing tales our hostess regaled us with whilst also savouring the splendour of our surroundings. We were being spoiled; how many people would have been lucky enough to have been scooped up by such a remarkable person, who not only was part of the establishment but possibly was the establishment!

After lunch, we were invited to tea with this lovely lady and encountered another experience which we hadn't bargained for. Why was that, I can hear you asking. Well she lived on the outskirts of town in what was possibly one of the first bungalows to be built in Mombasa by the early European settlers, and there were definitely no modern conveniences for this lady.

At the front of the bungalow there was a large veranda and there, sitting waiting for his memsahib, was her 'boy'. Actually, he was as old or older than his 'Mem' and had, I think, only a couple of teeth but a smile as big and welcoming as a full moon.

When he saw us he jumped up from his little stool and dashed off to make tea, whilst we were given a little history. It transpired that our lady had arrived in Mombasa on a bullock cart all the way from Nairobi, but was Scottish by descent, her husband being the first British judge to preside in Mombasa.

She had lived in the same house which, up until the demise of her husband, had no indoor sanitation. She regaled us with tales of having to wander down the garden path at night armed with a broom to frighten away all the snakes. What a to-do; I surely would never have lived to tell the tale!

Indoor sanitation was her only concession to modern living and, to prove the point, once tea had been served her lovely boy put the punka rope between his toes and we were then gently engulfed in a welcoming cool breeze.

It was time to take our leave and head over to the mainland via the amazing Mombasa ferry, which transported the world and his wife hither and yon.

Our next destination was Whitesands, a hotel situated on the palm fringed shores of the Indian Ocean. Now this was going to be the stuff that dreams were made of, and I was sure it would be simply idyllic. I will let you know!

Happy days – so in love!

Idyllic Days!

We spent an idyllic few days at Whitesands enjoying days that only dreams were made of. The hotel was built in a colonial style, the outside being wooden clapboarding that was painted white, which was typical of the region. It had large verandas that almost touched the palm trees as they swayed to and fro in the southerly winds.

The sheer beauty of the vista was so picture book perfect that it took one's breath away. We gazed out upon miles and miles of silken golden sands that were lapped by an azure blue sea, which was perfectly mirrored by the blue of the sky and, to complete the picture, there was not a cloud to be seen.

The palm trees made music whilst swaying in the balmy breeze and way out on the horizon, well beyond the reef, a dhow could be seen bobbing up and down to the ebb and flow of the tide, possibly heading for Dubai and no doubt laden down with exotica or maybe contraband from Zanzibar or India.

What a vista, we could have stayed there daydreaming forever and, in doing so, become the modern day equivalent of Mr and Mrs Robinson Crusoe. No chance, we had a date! Yes, a very special date. With whom? Hopefully some real live lions, so it was time to head off.

Our next stop was Tsavo National Park, where we were booked into Kilaguni Lodge for a few days, but we had to get there. Call us stupid or intrepid, as you will, but we reckoned we would hire a car and drive ourselves, as Tsavo was just off the Mombasa/Nairobi road — a doddle!

We sallied forth and were soon batting along the main road at a rate of knots looking out for a signpost for Voi, the turning off for Tsavo. Guess what car we had hired — a Volkswagen Beetle, at that time a favourite of mine. In retrospect, it was a silly choice; a tank would have been preferable.

At last we spied the turning, checked in with the ranger and literally headed into the bush. We had the feeling that we were being watched and, sure enough, looking down on us from a great height was an enormous giraffe. He was nonchalantly gnawing at a huge tree, possibly thinking to himself, whilst having a quiet chuckle, 'Here's another couple of ill-equipped tourists, posing as big white hunters. They sure don't know what they are letting themselves in for'.

We soon discovered how right he was, as from his perch way above us he could see what must to him have been a hilarious cameo that was about to unfold. He sure was going to have the last laugh at our expense! As they say, ignorance is bliss but, in our case, not for long as we were just about to receive the shock of our lives because round the next bend we were stopped in our tracks by a real live elephant. He was just standing there blocking our path; wasn't he big! But was he big, or was our Beetle a little small?

What to do now? Mike put the car in reverse as fast as he could and we careered backwards, missing a tree by inches. We sat there, actually quite terrified, as he was awfully big! I then suggested we hoot the horn. Well, why not, he was in our path. But Mike being the more sensible one reckoned we should lie low and hope that he would be on his way shortly. Also, he was a little larger than us – I didn't really need reminding of this fact – and if we annoyed him then one flick of his enormous trunk would send us into kingdom come, so with that I became a little less vociferous.

What had we let ourselves in for this time? We played a waiting game and eventually were able to proceed along this bumpy bush track, not having a clue on God's earth as to where we were heading and, more importantly, what or whom we might encounter en route.

The vegetation on either side was quite dense and high; consequently, it was like driving through a tunnel and very eerie indeed. Every time we came to a fork in the road we desperately hoped that there we would see a sign for Kilaguni Lodge. It took a while but, at last, oh the joy, we saw a notice detailing that the lodge was about ten minutes away, thank goodness. Even after this short time in a game park I wasn't too sure whether I was really up to morphing into a 'big white game hunter' — it was better to keep those thoughts to myself though!

We were now beetling along merrily, presuming that at least we were heading for a safe haven, and there it was round the next corner, wonders will never cease. We had arrived at a wooden building which had a big reception area opening onto a wide terrace, laid out with tables and chairs for relaxing and dining. Afternoon tea was being served, for which we were grateful. Suitably refreshed, we were shown to our room. Obviously, being our first time on safari, we hadn't readily appreciated that the accommodation in these lodges would be a little spartan.

Our room, like all the others, was off the main terrace and resembled a wooden garden shed. We entered to find two single beds each engulfed in the most enormous mosquito net. An adequate bathroom adjoined the room and that was it, very basic indeed.

We now had a couple of hours before changing for dinner, so off we trotted to enjoy a sundowner on the veranda and acquaint ourselves with our new home. We were amazed to find that the veranda was really not very wide with a wall possibly three or four feet tall separating it from the savannah, and consequently whilst dining one would have an uninterrupted view of the comings and goings of the animals.

There was a small lake surrounded by trees ahead of us and adjacent to the wall a salt lick had been constructed, which obviously would encourage the animals to wander in and partake of this delicacy right in front of our noses. As it was still daylight, it was hard for us to imagine how this tableau would unfold; we would have to be patient.

It was now time to bathe and dress for dinner. Yes, as hard as it might seem in today's casual world, in those days even in the 'bush' one dressed for dinner, with Mike wearing a lounge suit and I a dinner dress. Yes, attire more suitable for dinner at the Ritz but we were going to be dining at the Ritz of Tsavo, a restaurant with a difference, which boasted a cabaret the likes of which we could hardly begin to imagine, entitled the 'Folies Bergère' of the bush.

Off I went, only to find the door of our 'cabin' covered in geckos. Being faint-hearted I rushed back to Mike so he could ward them off. Job done, I gingerly entered. Yes, I know I was a wimp!

I tentatively ventured inside and proceeded to run a bath, only to get the fright of my life as there waiting for me was the most enormous bullfrog sitting in the middle of it, grinning from ear to ear. I just about had a heart attack; my goodness, the second in a matter of moments. Once again, I fled to find my man, with the broomstick. Oh God, it was a jolly good job I wasn't starkers! This time he had to stay and stand guard to repel any other unwanted intruders. What a ninny I was!

Once we were suitably suited and booted we returned to the veranda for more sundowners and dinner. By this time dusk had fallen and, to our amazement, search lights were illuminating the salt lick, pond and vegetation beyond. The scene was being set for the major attraction of the night.

We were told that soon we would see the most exciting spectacle ever and, sure enough, to our left a crocodile of elephants appeared through the trees, making their way to the salt lick. They trundled along in a single file, with the matriarchs heading the procession followed by the rest of the family right down to the newborns. There were maybe twenty or more in this contingent. Yes, a once in a lifetime spectacle, breathtaking in its simplicity and purity, and we were privileged to be only a few feet away enjoying the most marvellous dinner too, and all by the light of the silvery moon.

We were awestruck but as the animals padded away into the bush so did we to make sure we were bright-eyed and bushy-tailed for tomorrow's adventure. I was wary about entering our 'cabin' so my 'big game hunter' had to go first. When the coast was clear I entered, but that was after even my bed had been inspected for intruders! This was our first experience of sleeping under mosquito nets, and negotiating one's way through them took a bit of doing but obviously their presence was a necessity.

We were soon in the land of nod, or was it elephants, when I woke with the most enormous start as I was convinced a monkey had just landed on top of me. What a fright! Trying to disentangle myself from under the net was a nightmare but I had to get away rapidly. I threw myself on top of Mike's bed, but he too was entangled in a bloody mosquito net. Yes, you have guessed correctly, it wasn't me who padded about the room looking for a stray monkey, or was it monkeys? This experience, together with the blood-curdling noises coming from the bush made me realize that I would never, ever make a big game hunter!

Was I pleased to see the sun rising over the savannah, heralding the arrival of a new and, hopefully, less eventful day? My nerves were in tatters! Get me out of here!

Nervous Wreck!

To say I was a nervous wreck would be an understatement. I was a total quiver wondering just what wild animals might rear their ugly heads in or under my bed, and it did not take me long to register that I really was not cut out for this safari lark.

Oh, to be sauntering along the pavements of Knightsbridge anticipating a marvellous morning in my alma mater, Harrods, culminating in a delectable lunch in their Georgian Restaurant, which would surely include a plate of their finest rare roast beef. Dreams, dreams!

This would never do. I was there and it was the present, which meant partaking of breakfast overlooking the salt lick, but this time there were no animals in sight — perhaps they were having a snooze!

We needed to make a plan. But where to start? It was the pair of us, a Volkswagen Beetle and a map of Tsavo — we must have been mad.

We nonchalantly sauntered into the reception area, where all our fellow diners were being marshalled into groups. Without exception they looked the part, attired from top to toe in safari gear, complete with bush hats, cameras and binoculars draped around their necks.

Their expressions were of pure wonderment as they tried to anticipate what game they were about to see. Whereas we must have looked somewhat like Tweedledum and Tweedledee wondering just how we were going to mastermind our morning, see some game and hopefully not frighten ourselves witless into the bargain. I think we were being over optimistic!

We trailed after the safari groups who were whooping along in anticipation, saddled up the Beetle and drove out of the gates. Left, right or straight ahead? Did it matter? We beetled along, pardon the pun, sighting lots of game, like Thomson's gazelles, monkeys who were darting hither and yon, eagerly wondering whether they could hitch a ride, zebras, giraffes and, of course, elephants.

We zigzagged our way along the dusty red coloured dirt tracks, straddled by thorny bushes and gnarled old trees, which then gave way to savannah stretching as far as the eye could see, and there were animals everywhere, what a surprise!

It was a little monotonous really for poor Mike, who loves animals, as he was unable to take his eyes off the road for fear of coming face to face with something larger than us; actually that wouldn't have been too difficult! Naturally, we couldn't get out to change places for me to drive, for fear of being eaten alive. It reminded me somewhat of Hampton Court Maze, except for the fact that it was four-legged animals we were encountering and not two, and it was definitely more hair-raising.

We continued meandering around for a while and then spied the safari jeeps ahead, which had stopped and we were about to discover why. Oh my God, just beside us was a family of lions basking in the sun, and we both nearly died of fright on the spot.

What to do now? Actually we stopped and stared, reckoning that this was definitely a once in a lifetime experience, if our nerves could cope! We didn't think it prudent to hang about for too long though and plucked up courage to pass, without incident thank goodness.

We made a beeline over to the safari jeeps; my goodness, we were so relieved to now have some moral support. As might be imagined, they were understandably more than astonished to see this Beetle hurtling in their direction at breakneck speed.

Unlike us, who were only armed with a Brownie camera, their ranger was poised with a rifle to defend them to the last. We were so glad he recognized that we weren't a new species of wild animal!

From then on, we tagged along behind as they also had a 'game spotter' and consequently we were able to benefit from the guide's local knowledge and expertise, although we were a little low-slung to enjoy the bigger picture. We did arrive back at the lodge in one piece, which was no mean achievement. We awarded ourselves a resounding ten out of ten, but was that for stupidity for embarking on this stunt in the first place?

The rest of the day was spent idling around chatting to fellow guests, who were mostly Americans, anticipating the late night show at the salt lick. Would we see those marvellous elephants once again languidly sauntering in stage left, Tsavo's dancing boys and girls? We were now able to look forward to the moment because we knew there was a wall between them and us; how pathetic can one be.

Yes, I was glad when the time came for us to depart as we were heading for Nairobi once again to enjoy another night at the Norfolk Hotel, much more my style. At least there was no fear of a frog in the bath, geckos on the walls and maybe a monkey on the bed; I could sleep in peace! Sweet dreams.

The following morning we were up with the larks as we had an early start — not content with one stab at getting eaten by wild animals we decided to go for 'gold' and have another bash. Obviously, no visit to East Africa would have been complete without visiting the famous Treetops Hotel, where Princess Elizabeth had been staying when she heard of the death of her beloved father.

This time we had booked a mini trip, with the first stop being Treetops and the second the Outspan Hotel, which nestled under Mount Kilimanjaro. Both of these hotels where situated in the Aberdare National Park. Off we went along with half a dozen equally excited Americans, not knowing what to expect, as it was hard to imagine staying in a hotel built in the trees.

On arrival, we were greeted by a real life big game hunter, who explained that he was there to assure our safe passage whilst walking from the parking area to the tree house. Yes, this definitely was a walk on the wild side! I think the Americans were utterly bemused but there we were and off we went with one hunter leading the way and one following behind our little crocodile, both brandishing rifles. What we would have done if a lion had darted through the trees goodness only knows; had a collective heart attack I would guess!

Once we had crossed this grassy Rubicon we had to climb up a rickety ladder to reach the entrance to the house. The building was roughly hewn out of wood, which was quite an amazing feat of ingenuity, and needless to say there was nothing remotely five star about it. Actually, it reminded me of 'the house that Jack built'! Having negotiated the precarious climb, we entered into a large lounge/dining room which had observation windows along one side and there, taking centre stage, was an enormous mahogany table where our meals were to be served.

The room looked out onto a clearing in the woods and there before us were animals already partaking of a little substance from the salt lick. Now this place was definitely a game spotter's paradise!

We had a wash and brush-up in our room, which incidentally was more like a ship's cabin but instead of a porthole there was a lookout to enable one to sit, watch and photo the animals to one's heart's content.

We explored and found that the top deck was open, also looking down onto the lick and further beyond but, to our surprise, we were not alone but sharing the space with over-friendly monkeys, darting hither and yon. This was a little too upfront and personal as far as I was concerned. What to do? We couldn't really take off as we were effectively prisoners marooned until our big white hunter reappeared to offer us safe passage out.

This was surely very special, truly a once in a lifetime experience. To be privy to these animals' every movement without their knowledge was quite remarkable, and to think we were perched in a tree made it even more remarkable. We were all entranced, glued at the lookouts, so as not to miss a moment and we were not disappointed. Once dusk had fallen every imaginable species passed by, some tarrying and maybe sharing a gossip whilst enjoying a tasty bite and others just meandering through. The only sounds were of the animals slurping at the waterhole, grunting noisily or just stomping by. What a privilege to be privy to this tableau; it was surely a night to remember.

It was daybreak, with the noises of the night long gone, and now it was time for the birds to serenade us whilst enjoying our last moments in what must be one of the most special and unique hotels in the world.

The monkeys had the last laugh making their presence felt to the very end and, once we had departed, no doubt they would regroup readying themselves to run rings around the next visitors to enter their enchanted kingdom.

We were now off to spend a couple of days at the Outspan Hotel, which was also in the Aberdare National Park. To get there we drove through coffee and tea plantations, a vastly different terrain. We were going to the Outspan because it was just below Kilimanjaro and another 'must' on this African adventure.

We arrived at the Outspan Hotel, which was a very imposing building, and were immediately reminded that we were now light years away from the 'bush'. Our room looked directly onto Mount Kilimanjaro, which was topped with glistening snow and was a majestic sight. How different this was; we could have been in a vast country house in Scotland, what with the magnificent view, its wood panelled walls, huge log fires, and draughty corridors, and it was surrounded by glorious gardens stretching as far as the eye could see.

Surely this amazing house must have been a wonderful home and brought so much happiness to a pioneering family all those years ago. It was a real home away from home.

We were ready to depart, taking with us so many wonderful memories and cherishing all the experiences we had been lucky enough to have been offered. What a wonderful country.

What a Year!

It was not 'what a day it has been' but 'by Jove, what a year'. In fact, a total of fourteen months had elapsed since we left that green and pleasant land we used to call home, and now we were at Nairobi Airport waiting to be transported back from whence we came, all those moons ago!

Even a fortune-teller, looking into her crystal ball, couldn't have foreseen what a life changing year it was going to be for us. On reflection, that was possibly a good thing!

This time everything was tinged with excitement together with, I'm sure, a little apprehension. It was so different from that sad journey we undertook all those months ago. Who would have believed the change? There we were standing in the Kenyan sunshine with smiles on our faces, brimming with excitement, and added to this we had acquired a new found confidence that would have been impossible to imagine when that first journey was undertaken.

Last but by no means least, all the amazing tales we had to regale anyone who would listen. I was so sure we would not know where to begin and would possibly bore those we encountered rigid, but I bet we wouldn't care!

We boarded the Lufthansa flight bound for London via Frankfurt and, to the uninitiated, airline travel was blissful in those far-off days. If I recall correctly, there were only about twenty passengers on board the plane, which had the capacity of 275, or thereabouts. It was a far cry from today's pack them in and sell them cheap experience and, possibly, if you have the temerity to complain maybe they would threaten to throw you overboard!

Travel then was an exquisite experience with one's every wish anticipated and always catered for; those definitely were the days.

After a feather-bedded journey we were met by family and friends, just like royalty really, and then whisked off to Oxshott where Mike's parents lived. It did not take too long before we realized that even in the short time we had been away we had, in fact, fundamentally changed. A psychologist would have predicted that this transformation would have been inevitable in order to be able to adapt and survive in one's new habitat, but it came as a bit of a shock.

At the beginning of our year I had dreamt of this moment so many times and now it was here I wondered just what all the fuss was about. Yes, as they say, on many an occasion it is better to travel hopefully than to arrive.

You see inevitably everything was just how we had left it on that fateful morning but we had changed, on reflection, more than we could ever have imagined. We had been hurled into a frenetic and fast moving environment and had returned to a place where time had stood still.

Now that was something that had never crossed our minds when we were preparing for our homecoming, and our reaction astounded us. It proved that the old saying 'it's difficult to go back' is, after all, very apt.

Once the initial excitement had died down we were able to make a few plans. As luck would have it we were able to return to our house, which was great, as it enabled us to take up the reigns from whence we had left off. It was lovely catching up with our chums, visiting old haunts and quietly comparing our now two very different lives; it was all a little bewildering.

Actually, I think we became a little confused and I kept wondering where my Mohammed was! It had completely slipped my mind how to make a bed! What an admission!

To add to this mix, in our absence, my parents had moved from Surrey to a little village just outside Brighton and we had to be given a map in order to find them, which was all a little unnerving. As Dubai was considered a hardship posting we had the luxury of two months' leave and, once we had found our 'sea legs', began cavorting around like a couple of swells enjoying ourselves enormously.

Another pleasure and an unheard of phenomenon was that we actually had money in the bank. On reflection, we could honestly say it had been a very successful year. As the saying goes, in the end it turned out nice!

My chums would have thought there was something wrong if I hadn't hit the shops running and this time around I wouldn't make any awful mistakes, would I? I now knew what type of outfits would cut a dash and definitely what should not be entertained at any cost.

It was an altogether exhilarating experience purchasing long flowing little numbers, fashioned out of beautiful Liberty prints, some given added panache with details such as exquisite braiding and maybe hoods lined in contrasting colours — dresses that I'm sure even the Queen of Sheba would have been happy to wear. By the way, there wasn't a dress and jacket in sight let alone a pair of white gloves; a lesson had been learnt and now caution had definitely been thrown to the wind!

I also had one more very important date and that was with the uniform section of BOAC at Heathrow Airport to be issued with my uniform. My goodness, what a red-letter day that was going to be!

I duly arranged an appointment and was given directions to the uniform store, which seemed to be situated plonk in the middle of Heathrow and sounded a little hair-raising. I must admit it was somewhat scary driving alongside the main runway and it was certainly imperative to keep an eye out for planes taxiing in, as guess who would have had right of way and who could have ended up a sticky mess!

Amazingly, I arrived in one piece and was issued with the latest standard summer/tropical kit. This consisted of two navy shift dresses, two pink dresses and two turquoise ones, a regulation scarf, handbag, shoes, hat and the dreaded white gloves — I just couldn't get away from them!

I was in seventh airline hostess heaven! Who would ever have thought that I would be returning to Dubai not only as a seasoned expat but as a budding BOAC ground hostess to boot?

This time I couldn't return fast enough. There surely must be a moral to this story which possibly goes like this, 'Somewhere over the rainbow bluebirds fly. Birds fly over the rainbow. Why then, oh why can't I?' Now my dream was coming true and I would soon become a bluebird too!

We were now well and truly in the swing of this leave thing and dashing about hither and yon. Having bought up half of Surrey, I was once again buying up most of London and, together with family and friends, drinking the pubs dry! Now that's what I called living life to the full.

As previously mentioned, it had only taken a short twelve months for us to be seduced by our new found way of life, after our very tricky start. On reflection, we would have been a very sorry pair if that had not been the case.

I'm sure we must have sounded utterly preposterous, boring everyone silly with what we thought were frightfully funny stories! Even if our chums couldn't understand what we were wittering on about I'm quite sure it was evident that we had, without a doubt, embraced everything that the 'bloody abroad' had thrown at us and leafy Surrey was but a distant memory.

Before we return to Dubai, I must just mention Brighton where, in our absence, my parents had decamped, actually to a small village on the outskirts. Once we had located and become acquainted with this charming new outpost in our lives we were captivated.

My parents were real adventurers and were revelling living in a village which nestled under the Sussex downs entertaining glorious views of the sea, and were also gobbling up the delights that Brighton had to offer, which by any stretch of the imagination was rather a lot.

My goodness, what sophistication and charm it exuded. It surely was then, and still is, a unique city and it wasn't too long before we were calling it 'home'. In those days, Brighton was really very genteel although it has always had a risqué side which has given it an edge.

The little streets that made up the Lanes, winding their way up from the seafront, were captivating, very quaint and had barely changed from years gone by. Their real claim to fame though were the intriguing antique shops which abounded, and which were always stuffed to the gunnels with priceless objets d'art, with their owners being equally priceless characters too. I'm sure, given half the chance, they could and would have sold a bucketful of sand to the Arabs any day of the week.

In those days antiques weren't my thing but jewellery was and, surprise, surprise, the lanes were host to some amazing jewellery shops too. This was obviously going to be another good shopping destination for me and most unexpected; what a lucky girl I was! From what I had experienced so far, this enchanting place called Brighton was definitely living up to its reputation of London by the sea, and shaping up rather well, I would say!

Our departure beckoned but this time we had a spring in our step and a smile on our faces; yes, what a difference a year can make.

There was no fuss, no bother, just the two of us and mountains of luggage. We now knew the ropes so there were no nasty surprises. The plane, as usual, was virtually empty because by now you will have realized that most people in their right minds were hell-bent on avoiding an invitation to visit such a 'hotspot' other than doting parents, like mine! Now that definitely is another story!

Wet Kipper!

Here we were again, but this time with a smile on our faces, tingling with excitement and anticipation, wondering just how our second year in this desert kingdom would unfold.

It was simply amazing to be landing in Dubai, one year hence, and now thinking of the place as our adopted home, although we were not too sure who had adopted whom! Wonders will never cease!

The plane taxied up the runway, finally coming to a halt in front of one of the amazing whirligigs which protruded from the main airport building; these heralded the gateway to Dubai.

How avant-garde they were and, even in those far-off days, what a statement Dubai was making to the outside world. The gauntlet was surely being laid down, announcing the arrival of the newest, quirkiest kid on the construction block. Little did we know that over the ensuing years that blueprint would become the benchmark for some of the most exquisite architecture in the world, let alone Dubai.

The doors of the plane where flung open and in rushed that humid warm air; yes, the same warm air that we experienced and had recoiled from a year ago, but now we likened it unto Dubai's calling card.

One waft of that stifling heat together with its all engulfing humidity actually could be likened to being swiped by a nasty wet kipper, which said it all. Yes, we were home and ready for action. No words were required, we just savoured the moment. Lead on McDuff!

We grabbed our bags, laden with the spoils of war, I jest not. They were stuffed full of so many 'must-haves' and represented many, many hours of dedicated whizzing round and round, shop after shop, buying everything in sight. Our bank account was a little lighter than when we left these shores, but boy what fun I had had, and was I going to cut a dash at those parties! You bet!

Magically, Mohammed was there to greet us upon our arrival at the apartment. Yes, I think he was pleased to see us although his workload would escalate dramatically as now his holiday was over too. I was so pleased to see him, oh the joy, no more making beds or anything else for that matter on the domestic front!

It felt like home. Now that came as quite a surprise and was a little unexpected, as on reflection what we thought had been such a tricky twelve months couldn't have been so bad after all, unless we had developed amnesia, or once again had had a touch of the sun!

Once our greetings were over, we dashed onto the balcony to take in the magnificent view of the Creek which it afforded us. We were reassured; nothing had changed in our absence, and we were rewarded with the sound of the water gently lapping around the dhows, surely one of the most distinctive sounds of downtown Deira.

The twinkling lights from the mosque and the Majlis on the far side of the Creek were dancing on the water creating a kaleidoscope of colour that changed with the ebb and flow of the tide. This, together with the aromas that were wafting upwards from the giant cooking pots which were precariously balanced on the decks of the dhows, all added to the 'cameo' which shouted we were 'home'. That special picture abides to this day, not only for us but, I am sure, for so many who had also been privileged to enjoy that special moment.

Actually, it was so exciting that all my anxieties had vanished and I was relishing the chance to throw myself into everything my adopted 'home' of Dubai could offer. I was soon to discover that was so much more than I would ever have imagined a year ago. It was obviously no good becoming older, even if it was only by a year, and not getting a little wiser; oh how sage! Little did I know at that stage that this year was going to prove to be yet another turning point in my life.

Mike was immediately back at work and, consequently, getting up at an ungodly hour to be ready to leave at 6.30am and, as at this time I had lots to do too, I was sort of up with the larks as well.

Firstly, I gingerly unpacked my BOAC uniform, marvelling at the fact and gazing in wonderment that I, Jan, a married lady, could be embarking on another new journey equally as unexpected as the first one. Why was that? Well, at that time it was most unusual for married women to be working for BOAC as hostesses, whether it be in the air or on the ground, but as single European women were a bit thin on the ground in those days in Dubai Lady Luck played a hand.

I will tell you a little secret. When I met Mike I had the enrolment papers for BOAC in my handbag, but I was so bowled over by his charms they were never posted! Now there's a thing.

I had been told by the BOAC District Manager to contact him on my return. Oh, I did so hope he hadn't changed his mind or recruited somebody else in my absence. I apprehensively lifted the phone and, hey presto, was told everything was in order and was invited for a briefing to their offices. These were in the Dubai National Air Travel Agency, or DNATA, building not too far away, actually sort of left and just beyond the next sandy patch in the road.

My excitement knew no bounds; I arrived on the dot of 10am the next morning, where I was briefed as to what my duties would be. I would be on parade six mornings a week from 8am until 12 noon and would be reporting to the BOAC Airport Manager. I would have a mixed set of duties, a little bit of this and a little bit of that. I think the usual name for this type of job description is Girl Friday, but this Girl Friday was instructed that she had to wear the regulation uniform at all times, which included a jaunty hat and black stockings, indeed! And I wasn't even auditioning for the Folies Bergère!

I rushed back to the apartment not being able to believe my luck and, naturally, everywhere I looked took on a new identity. The dhows looked pristine, the coolies looked happy, and it really wasn't so hot, was it? And the sand wasn't flying all over the place; if it was I didn't notice. Those rose tinted glasses were working overtime! Nothing really mattered; yes, I was as happy as the proverbial sand boy!

I was going to start my job at the beginning of September but there was one slight hitch — how did I get to the airport? The airport was about two kilometres out of town, with the only known means of transport to get there being Shanks's pony or possibly a camel, and neither option appealed! Especially not togged up in my spiffing new uniform.

There was only one option, I had to have a car but in those days second-hand cars were quite a novelty. Why, you ask. Well, it wasn't so long ago when the usual mode of transport had four legs and two humps, maybe slightly superseded by pickup trucks but nothing much in the saloon range. These obviously would not have been considered as they really were no good for traversing all those sand dunes!

What to do? We then had a brainwave. There was a ramshackle alleyway near the airport where lots of mechanics plied their trade, fixing and mending anything and everything. We struck lucky because there before our eyes was the oldest and dirtiest VW Beetle we had ever seen, happily sitting there waiting for my arrival. About the only redeeming feature this vehicle had was that it possessed four wheels and the engine worked — it was love at first sight!

Oh, but the colour, it was battleship grey. Undeterred, we meandered around and found a paint spraying outfit, who were eager to oblige. Insanely I decided to have it sprayed bright orange; what statement I was trying to make I will never know, but boy, I reckon it could have been spotted from Mars, it was so bloody bright!

Once seen, never forgotten! No doubt I would live to rue the day as going anywhere incognito would definitely be out of the question, but at the time that thought never crossed my mind!

Everything was now in place for the big day, and I had two weeks to wait. In the meantime, Mike had settled back in and his Bitumen Supply Company was operating splendidly. His little bitumen tankers were plying up and down the Gulf, happily collecting bitumen from Khorramshahr, which was way up the Shatt al-Arab River in Persia.

They then retraced their steps, disgorging their cargo hither and yon along the way.

This was the very same bitumen that was being used to transform those desert tracks between Dubai and Abu Dhabi into a two-lane highway.

Unbeknown to all of us, that was definitely a little piece of history in the making and the foundations of today's Dubai. Amazing!

A happy face

No More Tears!

They say familiarity breeds contempt but I think, for me, now that I knew what to expect on a daily basis, my life seemed so very much easier. I wasn't constantly worrying and wondering and saying to myself, 'what if fate hadn't intervened; would I have been any happier in that green and pleasant land from which I had been catapulted?' Yes, I had now quietly come to terms with living in this sandy place, so no more tears!

Now there were no more real anxious moments, there seemed to be a constant buzz in the air. Yes, at long last, this place that we now called home beckoned us into its fold with her little finger saying, 'please enjoy, I know outwardly I don't have too much to offer but be patient and you will be rewarded'.

Yes, I was already feeling upbeat, especially when I took a quiet look at my super-duper uniform which was laid out on the bed in the spare room, realizing that it was mine and that I would soon be all togged up in it and ready for the off. Now that was an amazement in itself!

The apartment was running well and Mohammed was now quite an accomplished cook, especially at producing Sunday type lunches. Why is it that we British always stick so rigidly to our tried and tested menus? Is it because we are so set in our ways, or because our tuck is so jolly good?

It was now approaching the middle of September and all those who had fled away from the summer inferno had returned and the party whirl was being cranked up. We were all eager to share our summer stories with whoever would listen, and most definitely try and outdo each other; yes, that's girls for you! We were eager to show off our new purchases, which were waiting to be paraded around town as soon as the next gilt-edged invitation had been received.

It was now the eve of my debut as a ground hostess at the airport and I was excited and anxious in equal measure. In all honesty, it had seemed like a good idea at the time but how was I ever going to morph into a BOAC girl overnight? I think I was getting a touch of the jitters.

To say the least, I was somewhat nervous that morning, being all fingers and thumbs whilst trying to dress, and once I had accomplished the task I didn't recognize the person staring at me in the mirror, what a transformation!

I was dressed in the turquoise shift dress, black stockings and navy shoes, together with the air hostess type hat perched on my head, which I had given instructions to not to fall off, as it would most certainly ruin the picture! Would you believe, I was even clutching a little pair of white gloves and, last but not least, the regulation handbag slung over my shoulder. Yes, looking back at me from the mirror that morning was a poster picture of an airline hostess in the early seventies and it was me, wonders will never cease!

I was ready for the off. This was it, there was no turning back! My wonderful bright orange Beetle awaited me, now all I had to do was summon the lift. Mohammed's, the janitor, eyes nearly popped out of his head when he spied me alighting from the lift. I would also imagine that most of the deckhands from the dhows across the road must have almost fallen into the Creek, never before having seen such an apparition, attired as I was, ever before in their lives.

It only took minutes to get to the airport, passing the Clocktower roundabout as I went. It would be very hard to imagine now, but I think there were possibly only about six other cars in the vast car park; now that was Dubai Airport in 1971!

I slowly climbed the steps and walked across the concourse to the BOAC office. Now I really have to paint the picture here. In those far off days, the actual traffic that went through the airport was minimal, and BOAC only operated three passenger flights per week from London, sometimes disgorging fewer than ten passengers. Consequently, the concourse was usually nigh on deserted, and only managed a little spark when BOAC were operating to London and Middle East Airlines to Beirut. Yes, it's so very hard to imagine, I know!

I gingerly knocked on the door, which was opened by the BOAC Airport Manager, whom I had not met. He was enormous, formidable and sported a beard, which was slightly reddish in colour. The office over which he presided was where all aircraft movements that were operated or looked after by BOAC were managed. I was to discover that this little room was the logistical 'powerhouse' of BOAC's operation in Dubai.

He was ably assisted by two or three young trainees on secondment from London and now he had me too. Oh my goodness, neither he, nor I or the airport knew what we were in for.

The trainees were responsible for writing up flight plans for onward journeys, which entailed calculating the amount of fuel to be put on board once various elements had been taken into account, which obviously included wind speed, weather conditions en route and the weight being carried on board, an exacting task.

I was shown my desk, which took centre stage; there was definitely no hiding place here. I proceeded to try and make myself at home; my goodness, it was so very different from any offices I had previously worked in. For a start, we were all in uniform, with the boys looking very smart in theirs, which consisted of black trousers and white shirts, whilst the Station Manager sported gold epaulettes on his shirt, which denoted his seniority.

I was introduced and my duties explained. They didn't seem too onerous – making coffee, making more coffee, and logging all the stats which were filed about incoming and outgoing flights – but it was painfully obvious that I was going to have to get used to the office banter. Yes, I was normally the only girl about at this time of day and I had to quickly adjust to being the butt of many a little joke or jibe — one of the boys I had to become pronto, if I was to survive! Was I up to it? You bet!

Okay, the first day was a little daunting but the second was mind-blowing. I had to be in early as this was the morning I had sole charge of making sure the arriving and departing passengers were looked after. My instructions were to meet the flight from Bombay, look after the disembarking passengers and, as the plane was London bound, to look after the onward passengers as well. How does one meet a flight, somebody please help me?

I was in a blind panic, more so when I saw the VC10 taxiing in; I actually nearly died of fright. I was positioned at the arrival gate, rigid with fear, and watched the doors of the aircraft open and the passengers disembark. They then seemed to gallop up the whirligig towards me — I almost bolted! I somehow gathered my very scattered wits, smiled sweetly, collected their disembarkation cards and then made sure they were united with their luggage.

This first task was accomplished with no mishaps but I then had to dash off to my next assignment, and had forgotten what that was! This was a little like playing blind man's bluff, but who was blind and who was bluffing!

Oh yes, I knew it was to go to the check-in area, so off I dashed but, once there, had no clue as to what I was meant to do. It was very clear to me that I only had a couple of options: stand there like a ninny or smile sweetly and talk about the weather, although as the sun always shines in Dubai that was not too difficult!

Thank goodness I was not alone and found that the check-in area was ably manned by super chaps from DNATA, who were extremely capable and did all the important stuff, so I was saved. On that first terrifying morning, that was a good thing because I have my doubts that if I had had anything to do with this operation, these unsuspecting people would probably never have seen their luggage again.

They were lucky too as there was only one plane on the ground at the time, otherwise who knows where they might have landed up! Now you will be wondering just how many passengers I might have had to assist. It felt like a cast of thousands because I was so nervous, but it was possibly ten or maybe less.

As previously mentioned, not too many people had reason to visit Dubai in those early days in the seventies. In reality, it was an extremely exclusive club and, on reflection, we were the founder members.

My goodness how Topsy has grown!

Soft Shoe Shuffle!

What with now working at the airport every morning, and that was six mornings a week, my days had turned into something akin to the soft shoe shuffle. Why was that, I hear you asking.

Well, after yet another night out on the town, arriving home late and getting up early, shuffling along was the only option available, preferably in the slow lane! That is if one wanted to arrive at one's destination bright-eyed and bushy-tailed, although sometimes that was a tall order!

It's true to say I had taken to the job like a duck to water, loving every moment. Was it the buzz, was it the uniform or, my goodness perish the thought, was it being a token female at the airport every morning?

Or, maybe, it was being in charge of almost everything but with one notable exception and that was piloting the plane. It really was anybody's guess but a little bit of all three, I think! My goodness, what an intoxicating mix!

Each morning, when I had finished kitting myself out in 'that' new gear of mine, I would look into the mirror and would say, 'Is that yoo-hoo?' My goodness, what a transformation I had undergone and I loved it; mind you, who wouldn't?

One thing though, I still wasn't too adept at firmly securing that natty hat that perched like a bird's nest on top of my head, and I was constantly terrified that it would fly away just when I was trying to impress God knows who!

Everything was going really well. There were no catastrophes at the airport and so far I hadn't put anybody on the wrong plane, but there was always time! It surely was a godsend that there was normally only one plane on the ground during those morning shifts otherwise it might have been a question of 'eeny, meeny, miny, moe', and goodness knows where my passengers might have ended up!

In retrospect, the passengers in my charge during those hectic, happy days had a very lucky escape as they could have been in for a big surprise, and I could have been in for an even bigger surprise — a very high 'high jump'!

As they say, it was all a laugh and a giggle and it sure gave a new meaning to 'airport departures'. These occasions were very special indeed; it was VIP treatment all the way, even though it was all a little unorthodox.

We were now into early November when the humidity tended to be extremely high and dodgy cars, like my bright orange Beetle, had a tendency to succumb to this phenomenon, meaning it was very hard to start. I normally managed to cajole it into life but this particular morning was an exception as there wasn't a squeak out of it.

We didn't lack an audience though and eventually the farash and the boys from the dhows, which were moored opposite, jumped into action. Firstly, they gave it a shunt and then a shake and also checked the ignition   no joy. So with a great heave-ho they started pushing the Beetle, with me at the helm, round the corner.

We went past the front of the Oasis Hotel, along to Gray Mackenzies and then left past Red Shoe, until we eventually reached the main road, still with no sign of life — it was as dead as a dodo. What did we do now? They couldn't possibly push me all the way to the airport, could they?

Obviously it was quite beyond my remit as I only knew how to put the ignition key in the designated slot, turn the key and then whizz off up the road, with no worries.

That was my undoing, as one of these chaps had the extraordinary idea of checking the petrol gauge and, would you believe it, the tank was empty. I was incredulous. How could that be? As if I didn't know, what a dummy I was! And what a red face I had!

At that precise moment I was so very glad that my language skills left a lot to be desired and I couldn't understand Arabic, Urdu, Hindu or any other language you can think of, because they were not best pleased with little old me!

From that day on when they saw me charging out of the lift in the early mornings they always made themselves scarce and, to this day, I could never understand why! There is surely a moral to this little story — it would possibly be a very good idea indeed if, from time to time, I filled up the tank and I should also maybe enrol in a car mechanic's course, pronto! What do you think?

The farash still looked bemused and incredulous every time I popped out of the lift in my gear. These days though, the boys from the dhows were far more wily and they kept their heads down just in case they were required to help this maiden in distress, which would, without a doubt, require some terrible physical activity on their part, like pushing the Beetle halfway round town! Who could blame them?

What a sensation I was causing! But obviously, in my newly found exalted position I should really try and act with a little decorum; after all, I was 'flying the flag'!

Although I was still sailing most afternoons, I now had other priorities which were becoming more pressing. Would you like to know what these were? Well, we were now being invited to so many parties. Dubai seemed to have turned into one big party-go-round and, obviously, a girl needed the correct attire. Darling, one couldn't possibly be seen wearing the same outfit twice, well not in one week anyway!

Naturally, this necessitated many trips to the Textile Souk and the tailors, is that a surprise or is it a surprise! Actually, wandering around the Souk in the early evening was a truly magical experience as it was always a very special place to be at that time of day, and consequently this little exercise was always full of fun and promise.

One's tummy rumbled too with anticipation, hoping that it would get the chance to devour a magnificent shawarma because the aromas that were wafting around were too tantalizing for words.

Oh, what wonderful memories!

Sometimes though, time was of the essence as the party-go-round usually began at 7pm kicking off with cocktail or drinks parties. As there were still few hotels in Dubai which were deemed suitable to cater for such occasions they were usually held in private residences; in other words, the houses of the Number Ones. A truly lovely nickname for company bosses!

The few new homes that were being constructed in Dubai at that time were usually large, opulent and suitable to cater for such events; in other words, they were party houses. There was only one drawback though, and that was that these houses seemed to be built in the deep blue yonder and one usually had to wade through mounds of sand to get to the front door.

It was worth all the effort though as the first thing you saw when the door was opened would usually be two or three waiters lined up and offering the largest gin and tonic you could ever imagine this side of the next sand dune.

After quenching one's thirst, one would sigh contentedly and agree that, yes, the trek had really been worthwhile and also well rewarded. Let's have another one — I don't mind if I do!

Black Stockings!

I had taken to my newly found status of the 'only girl in the world', or I should say the only girl wearing black stockings, at Dubai Airport every weekday morning like a duck to water.

I quickly discovered that there was something about wearing a uniform which seemed to alter one's personality, as one instantly became part of a team and, actually, it also made one feel very important indeed.

Mind you, looks can be a little misleading because I seemed to be whizzing round in circles most of the time. Hopefully, though, looking as if I knew what I was doing, at least some of the time! Some hope, but it was worth a try!

It took a while to settle, as it was such a different working environment from the staid office set-ups that had been my norm, but I gradually got the hang of things. In most offices, there was usually little room for manoeuvre and, once inside the door, one was usually tethered to the desk for the duration.

I was able to wander around to my heart's content and nobody seemed to bat an eyelid, and the freedom suited me admirably!

On one particular jaunt I discovered that there were enormous kitchens in the basement, where Albert Abella's chefs prepared meals for the in-flight catering. Actually, that all sounds so grand but, as there were so few planes arriving and departing, they were not exactly overworked and their menus were only as exotic as the produce available in the local markets allowed.

My goodness, on occasions Chefie must have had a fearful headache wondering just what he was going to be able to conjure up with the meagre victuals he had at his disposal. He sure was a master of invention!

In those days, gourmet airline meals were not normally on the agenda — one ate to live, rather than live to eat. Actually, if I recall correctly, BOAC were always reluctant to upload food from the airport catering in those far off days; maybe they thought their passengers might have ended up eating a communal mutton grab!

And the terrifying spectacle of watching one lucky passenger being offered one of the most sought after delicacies known to man – yes, one of the animal's eyeballs – was too much to even contemplate, and I'm not sure who would have had a fainting fit first! Only joking, or am I?

Once the ice had been broken and I had become acquainted with Chefie and his crew it was amazing what little treats found their way back to our offices, via little old me. Actually, the whole tenor of the place reminded me of the Three Musketeers – all for one and one for all – except there were many more than three!

I could never figure out who d'Artagnan might have been, but surely I could have been cast as Maid Marian; oh, what fun it was turning out to be. Actually, on occasions it bordered on the farcical and, before you ask, no eyeballs ever found their way to the office, unless they were in disguise! Now there's a thought!

No morning was the same, as our office was the staging post for a cast of thousands, with pilots and their engineers passing through to either deliver or collect onward flight plans. Then there were the marvellous officers from RAF Masirah who visited Dubai on a weekly basis, bursting into the tiny office like Spitfires, with their handlebar moustaches twitching hither and yon. It went without saying that their visits caused utter mayhem and, yes, they all wanted coffee too!

Initially, it was all a little bemusing but, after a month or two, I was caught up in this mysterious web entitled 'the airline business'. The boys from RAF Masirah would bound in, looking for fun as they were usually in Dubai for a little R and R.

Masirah is an island off the coast of Oman in the Indian Ocean and, at that time, it was a staging post for military aircraft flying east, hence the deployment of military personnel. To say the least, the island was somewhat off the beaten track and the boys, I think, felt that they had been plonked into the deep blue yonder, hence their delight at the thought of being let loose in Dubai for a couple of days.

Normally, their first question was, 'When is the next VC10 due in for a stopover?' They were oh so subtle, I don't think. This was a coded question to find out if there might, just might be a few air hostesses floating about the place to be swept up by these 'gallant gentlemen'!

I was, of course, getting to know the boys too and, invariably, would invite them to drop into the apartment for sundowners or whatever. Consequently, it was not unusual for Mike to return to find the apartment invaded by lots of handsome strangers. Mind you, he soon got used to these surprises!

As our apartment was slap in the centre of Deira, it was turning into a 'downtown staging post' and soon began taking on a personality of its own. One of the reasons for this was that, naturally, they all knew they would receive a warm welcome and also, in those days, there were few coffee shops or bars where one could take refuge from the steaming heat, except – yes, right first time – Apartment 603.

Since we had no radio or television, listening to the antics of these chaps was the next best thing; a sort of Carry On show, always to be continued with each episode being more hair-raising than the last.

We were also being visited by the BOAC boys who flew freighters from London to Hong Kong via Dubai. As these were regular flights, they too became part of the family. Quite often they could be spied walking down the road from the hotel to the apartment lugging yet another piece of furniture I had asked them to buy in Hong Kong — camphor chests were a great favourite. We had them in every shape and size! And then there were the gold watches!

If it was not the odd trinket from Hong Kong, it was a little something from Marks and Spencer, as long as the labels were cut out! Yes, in those days it was a fate worse than death to arrive at the airport with even the smallest M and S label lurking in one's luggage; how times have changed! We were always quite terrified of being rumbled.

They now have numerous Marks and Spencer stores in Dubai; is that progress, or is it progress — yes, times have most definitely changed!

Everything now seemed to have a purpose because I was occupied. All was rosy in my world, and Mike's too, because at long last he didn't have to worry about me — well, not too much!

I was working in the mornings then sailing most afternoons, some days venturing under the Al Maktoum Bridge and way down to where the Municipality Building was eventually constructed. It was a wonderful feeling of total freedom, with the sun on my back and the wind in my hair. Who could have wished for anything more?

By now, I knew most of the boys at the sailing club and also, when a VC10 was overnighting, I became acquainted with these crews too or, more to the point, they all knew me. It was lots of fun and, as time went by, we became good chums.

I looked forward to these visits immensely. Mind you, it was hard to imagine that it was only a few months ago that I had been oh so lost and lonely, bereft of any company at all. It had taken these boys and girls, passing through to far-off places, to restore my equilibrium. They were heaven sent!

To the uninitiated, airports are mysterious places and it takes many different groups of people to ensure they operate and function safely.

One such group was IAL, International Air Radio Limited, and these boys operated the control tower. Consequently, they were responsible for the safe landing and departure of all planes, which was a very important job indeed. Now that I was part of this fraternity, I discovered that they were seasoned expats who travelled the world guiding planes safely in and out of airports from here to Timbuktu.

Their work was very exacting and once off duty they sure loved to party. We soon earned our stripes but had a lot of catching up to do, as these parties were very different from the genteel little drinks parties we were used to in leafy Surrey. Would you believe there was not a glass of sherry in sight!

We were also rubbing shoulders with the boys from the military fraternity in Sharjah, many being involved in covert operations. There were the TOS boys, the chaps from the Scots Guards doing six-month stints and, of course, the RAF boys — yes, it was boys, boys and more boys! Coffee mornings and ladies' lunches were but a distant memory; what a change of lifestyle! That was the understatement of the year!

Time and time again it was brought home to one that adaptability was definitely the name of the game, and the motto had to be 'give it a whirl, Shirl' or 'if you can't beat them, join them'. A valuable lesson had been learnt — it was called survival.

What a Duffer!

For once I was actually doing a job that I enjoyed and I really couldn't think why it had taken so long to discover that I was never cut out to be a secretary; in fact, it couldn't have been a worse choice of occupation for me. OK, it was my fault entirely because I didn't pay too much attention at school, finding it all somewhat stifling and, dare I say, a little boring; a daily grind that had to be endured!

Consequently, when it came to the next step in my life 'what to do with Jan' or, more importantly, 'what on earth could Jan do' secretarial college seemed to be the only answer. Oh dear, what a daft idea that was!

My mother seemed to be under the impression that any fool could master shorthand so presumably it wouldn't be too difficult for her duffer of a daughter to get to grips with the situation. Actually, with all due deference, she had no idea what she was talking about and couldn't understand why I thought it all rather beastly and so very difficult. Oh, I was so awkward and not a little insubordinate! What a surprise, it went without saying that I could never read my shorthand back and, in fact, it was a total disaster.

My year of studying to be the perfect secretary at times resembled a Greek tragedy and, unfortunately, I had been bequeathed the star part and that included how to master shorthand. I am convinced that this task must have been equally as difficult as mastering Greek! Maybe, though, Greek would have been an easier option!

Those days were now behind me and I was happily charging around in my BOAC uniform having the time of my life, and to think I could possibly have been doing this for years because we only lived a few miles from Heathrow Airport; I was obviously slow on the uptake! It necessitated embarking on a hair-raising posting to Dubai to realize my potential — well, that's how I saw it, although my new found work colleagues might have begged to differ.

As previously mentioned, Dubai Airport was brand new and almost futuristic in its design but very pleasing to the eye. Everything about it was light and airy but, naturally, it was always cool. The departure lounge was enormous, especially when one was reminded that BOAC only had three passenger flights a week and maybe only a handful of passengers boarding or disembarking at any one time. It really would have made an ideal play area of some description, or maybe a ballroom during its empty moments – and there were many – what fun that would have been!

Because of the intimate nature of the place, it did not take too long to get to know everyone. The ground staff at the airport all worked for DNATA and were mainly from India or Pakistan. There were some glorious characters in their midst and, would you believe it, they were all besotted with cricket, now there was a surprise!

To complete this cast of amazing characters were the sales representatives from the various airlines, an economic necessity. BOAC had a super chap working for them who was Lebanese; he was always wheeling and dealing, doing his level best to put bums on seats, and outwitting his rivals into the bargain!

On getting to know him though, it soon became obvious that he was my man if I needed to get my sticky paws on a couple of freebies. Somehow he always managed to spirit these up, like a rabbit out of a hat! Miraculous!

By now the golf course was a reality, albeit a little wobbly on its feet, instead of being that almost unimaginable dream that had been nursed by the golfing fraternity for so long.

This monumental achievement could surely be classified as one of the Seven Wonders of the World, particularly when one recalls just what an enormous undertaking it had been. What do they say, 'Everything comes to those who wait'?

Obviously, when one thinks of golf courses the colour green normally springs to mind. Now please close your eyes and what do you recall when thinking of your dream course? Yes, I know, billiard board greens, lush fairways and just a hint of sand in the various bunkers, blue skies, the sun shining, and birds twittering around and about — heaven!

Sadly, in this instance, you would be oh so wrong, so open those eyes and stop daydreaming. In fact, all you would see as far as forever would be sand, sand and glorious sand. No doubt you would say to yourself, 'Who is off their rockers, me or them?'

'Them' being the boys, including Mike, who revelled in the amazing challenge that this little piece of golfing heaven afforded them, whilst making sure they didn't accidently hit a passing camel; after all, it was only being curious!

Obviously, improvisation was the name of the game and the traditional 'greens' were morphed into 'browns'. This was achieved by oiling sand, after which it was rolled flat to create a flat putting surface. The greens of Wentworth they were not but remarkably they played very true. Naturally, they were the pride and joy of the golf course committee; so ingenious.

It transpired that this technique had been honed to perfection in East Africa and the idea brought to Dubai by the golf mad chaps who had been posted to Dubai from there. It was an amazing tale of 'where there's a will, there's a way', even though the way might be a little sandy and inundated with curious camels on occasions, but nobody really cared.

I recall that the first 'Club House' – such a grand name – was a Portakabin which morphed into a wonderful 19th hole, where the boys could quench their thirst and swap their marvellous golfing stories. Surely one of those stories had to be 'how a little bit of desert' had been tamed by so few for so many!

The Portakabin didn't last too long and, once sufficient funds had been acquired, work started on a permanent building. The Dubai Golf and Country Club was now definitely taking on a life of its own.

Unbeknown to us founder members, it was to become a very welcoming and happy refuge for many, many hundreds of expats over the course of time. Yes, like Topsy, it was to grow and grow.

There obviously had to be a 'golf' committee, which would also mull over the idea of what other sports could possibly be introduced in the fullness of time. With the best will in the world, other than building sandcastles, nobody had any idea what to do or how to do it, other than nurture the obvious next best sport on the agenda — 'happy hour' at the 19th hole.

It was soon realized that a Social Committee had to be formed as a matter of great urgency and, yes, guess who was elected onto the committee; yes, little old me! Between us 'girls' we had bright ideas, but exactly how they were going to be implemented was anybody's guess because for any function food normally played a big part and the kitchen was just being installed. Ah, but we were resolute and wouldn't let the lack of a kitchen dampen our resolve to put on the greatest soirée this side of the next sand dune! Well, that was the general idea!

We obviously needed an abundance of wit, help and guile to achieve our aim. Yes, would you believe, another nightmare was about to unfold and it wasn't all of our own making!

A Terrible Tale!

If you have been following my story, you will have noted that I have not recently mentioned another pastime, so enjoyed by many, and that is the dreaded card game of bridge. I had managed to avoid being drawn into a duel over a pack of 52 cards by ducking and weaving around the place, with great difficulty, I might add.

Consequently, it was inevitable that I wouldn't be able to outmanoeuvre the dreaded bridge playing ladies forever and one fateful day it happened, I was ensnared, much against my better judgement.

For those of you who are not familiar with this apparently genteel pastime, I kid you not, on occasions it can resemble an all-out civil war, and don't I know it because the first time I was captured, I think I was recruited as the cannonball!

On reflection, sometimes it was quite handy to have a scapegoat in one's midst, passing the buck, for possibly your own inadequacies. Although it was a very cowardly practice I would say, especially when you found yourself to be the said scapegoat!

I fell into the trap well and truly, and was caught on the hop by being invited to a 'bridge supper'. I protested, declaring that really my bridge capabilities were virtually non-existent, and also I had no time for such frivolities as I was too busy with my sailing. 'Don't be silly,' the host said in a frightfully haughty voice, 'we accommodate every level of player and, in any case, we need to make up numbers'. Oh dear, oh dear, I had that sinking feeling that my life could be spinning out of control.

Oh dear indeed, now what did I do? I simply have to remind you that in those far off days we only had a few modern amenities. A telephone, but only just, so it would surely be difficult to find a friend to give me a clue. Possibly lurking around Dubai there might have been a copy of the Encyclopedia Britannica but could one have gleaned any useful tips there?

Maybe there might have been a chapter on how to become a card shark in one easy lesson, or another on bluff and counter bluff. I wasn't too sure, but there was no time to find out anyway. I was on my tod. OK, Mike would be by my side but I seriously wasn't too sure what good that would do either!

I had nobody to ask for advice and, after all, Dubai was a very small place. It just couldn't be admitted that my card playing skills might be ranked on the Richter scale as possibly just above zero. What an admission that would be to those formidable card wheeling ladies; OK, I'd best keep quiet.

The day finally arrived; yes, I was literally quaking in my boots, praying for a sudden earthquake that would swallow me up. No such luck, so we sallied forth and eventually found the house, which was at the back of Deira, tucked away in the dark sandy streets.

The large Arab door was opened, which led into a very large space being the vestibule or, in Arabian parlance, the Majlis, which was a meeting room where people were milling around before making their way to the card tables. I was about to meet my Waterloo!

Our hostess was frightfully nice, if you know what I mean. 'Oh, how lovely to see you, my dear,' she chortled, 'now who don't you know?' Actually, squinting around, I came to the conclusion that I didn't know anyone and, at that moment, didn't want to either! Or maybe I had succumbed to a temporary bout of amnesia, which I hoped would last all night. Yes, that would do the trick!

My only hope was that they had mislaid the packs of cards, but no such luck. A voice boomed out, 'Please take a card. Check which number you are and on which table you are playing, where you should meet up with your partner for the first rubber'.

I stumbled off, found the table and was introduced to my first partner. I was simply terrified and totally lost for words. I hadn't a clue on God's earth what they were talking about or how to reply to their unfathomable questions and, when it came to 'What convention do you play?' I said, 'Usually the Chopin'.

Actually, I thought that was very funny, only to be met with withering looks from my partner and also the opposition. Did one call them that? More like the enemy!

The cards were shuffled, cut and dealt. Yes, I had thirteen but, as you will have detected, didn't have much idea what to do with them, save arranging them into suits, which I dutifully did. Now what? Ah yes, one needed points; how did you come by those? It then came to me that it was something to do with how many coloured jobs you possessed, but really didn't know how many points each represented.

Surely my partner would have had apoplexy if he had known what was going on, as to me he looked terrifying. So, I decided to stay mute, clutching the cards in my sweaty hands, gulping my gin and tonic thinking, 'It's not unlike being before the firing squad; please get it over with so I can be put out of my misery'.

No such luck. I stumbled around, shaking like a leaf, clutching the cards, dropping the cards, slurping too much gin, generally feeling exceedingly sorry for myself and, yes, out of my depth! Would the evening ever end? If it didn't end soon I may have had to make a dash for it!

Finally, after what seemed like a lifetime, we had changed tables many times, something akin to a terrifying game of musical chairs, only with no happy music to lift the spirits. We had played with the other pairs and now it was time for the prize giving. No surprises there.

I don't really want to go down that route, but is there such a position as minus last? Well, suffice to say there was that night! We bade our farewells and I dashed for the door as fast as my little legs would carry me. Once it was closed, I collapsed on the sandy road in tears — what a terrible disaster. I had felt like a pariah, unwittingly having stumbled into – or was it onto – an alien planet.

Well, Jan, that was another lesson learnt in the social minefield —
not to be bamboozled into anything, especially making up a fourth
at bridge, just because those terrifying women needed a fourth. You
realized that once you had acquiesced through the kindness of your
heart, all you would receive is abuse because you trumped your partner's
trick. Oh no, count me out!

I was still smarting the following morning but, being a well brought
up young lady, it went without saying that I had to phone our hostess.
But what did I say?

My dear, such a lovely evening, I so love playing bridge but – so
sorry – I seemed to have been a little off colour, or was it colour blind,
because I couldn't work out my hearts from my spades. As for those
'no trumps' I was looking for them all night but couldn't find them
anywhere, they must have landed up on the floor! Ah well, it's only a
game isn't it? It's obviously not too friendly though.

No, that wouldn't do. Maybe I could say I lost my glasses. Enough
of this, just pick up the phone and get it over with.

'Oh, hello,' she said, 'yes, the food was exceptionally good, wasn't
it; I have such a wonderful cook'. Lucky you, I thought!

That was before I had stuttered, 'I'm so sorry that I ruined your
bridge evening,' to which there was a deathly silence.

Then she lobbed what seemed like a hand grenade down the phone
by saying, 'You did know, didn't you, that the shortish chap wearing
glasses is an international player and plays in many tournaments around
the world?'

Oh my God, he was my first partner, no wonder he was giving
me pitying looks whilst playing, and also for the rest of the evening.
No doubt he would be thinking that having been bequeathed me as
a partner would have stopped him from scoring maximum points.
Consequently, he would have been unable to be crowned King of the
Castle for the evening, which would have dented his ego no end!

He would have been in the fortunate position, of course, of being
able to blame it on his partner; nothing to do with him at all, such is
the nature of this terrifying game.

Yes, the moral of this story is never fall for a sob story, especially when it involves making up a four at bridge because you know what the consequences will be. Yes, at the end of the session you will resemble a squashed fly — not a pretty sight.

You know you are happiest when pitting your wits against the elements in your sailing boat, being in charge of your own destiny. Always bear that in mind when you receive an invitation to make up a dreaded fourth at bridge.

Pass the Smelling Salts!

Oh my goodness, what had I let myself in for? It was all very well being willing to help but being bombarded with questions and phone calls was definitely another matter. Yes, I was now embroiled, like one of those beer can chickens stuck helplessly on top of a barbecue, but this was no barbecue — it was the Social Committee of the Dubai Country Club!

I knew we had some serious work to do, but this was ridiculous. I thought this would be fun but we now seemed to be responsible for everything including rumbling stomachs all round and, I might add, there were many.

The brief also included entertainment. How in God's name did you conjure up the equivalent of the Glenn Miller Orchestra halfway to the Empty Quarter, I ask you?

I obviously found myself on the wrong committee; this definitely was not a game for a laugh! Where were the smelling salts?

I will be honest, our first function left a lot to be desired, even though we all bragged that nothing was impossible and that, of course, we could put on a marvellous do without any real facilities at all – and by that I mean a kitchen – yes, we were a little naive, to say the least. We were so full of our own importance that we didn't give it a thought.

A date was fixed for the inaugural party, and with hindsight that was the easy bit. What did we do now?

We scratched our furrowed brows and pondered. Ah yes, we would cajole anybody and everybody to produce a plate of food. What a good idea — instead of passing the parcel it was passing the buck. In the end, all we would have to do was to wind up the gramophone and get the bar stocked up. Let the party begin!

The upshot was that there were plates and plates of soggy sandwiches, screechy music, and lots and lots of pickled golfers with us girls flying round and round in circles like demented red-faced bats, wishing to be anywhere but there!

A mighty lesson had been learnt and, for me, it was quite simple — keep your mouth shut and don't volunteer for anything! It will only get you into trouble!

Decision time. With immediate effect, no more social events were to be planned until the new kitchen was operational. The idea was welcomed by all and sundry, as nobody could bear the thought of another soggy sandwich!

The golf course had been embraced by everyone and, quite naturally, it didn't take long for it to become well and truly established, with the 'men' enjoying many a happy afternoon pitching and putting through the sand, and now they were being joined by the redoubtable ladies of the LGU.

For the uninitiated, the LGU stands for the Ladies Golf Union; yes, a truly formidable bunch of club wielding ladies who loved their golf too, and who were always ready to give the gentlemen golfers a run for their money!

What a happy playground that patch of sand at the head of the Creek was turning into. It just goes to show that one can't judge a picture by its cover. Surely it would have been impossible to find anything looking less like a conventional golf course on God's earth. It's the imagination that does it you know, together with an enormous amount of faith. Miraculously, there was an abundance of both!

As it was now coming up to Christmas and the real big-time party season was about to erupt, Mike and I thought we ought to show willing and give our first 'big bash'. And what did we come up with? Well, in a million years you will never guess — the Mad Hatter's Pimm's Party, black tie, of course!

The general idea was that suitably smart attire was required of tuxedos for the men and long dresses for the ladies, all to be topped off with mad hats. We must have become totally addled by the heat to have had such an idea! I blush even now thinking about it and the consequences it had!

Naturally, we thought the whole idea simply hysterical and, in retrospect, it was because the Pimm's was our secret weapon. You probably know that the recipe for a good Pimm's is normally one bottle of Pimm's to a third of gin together with the necessary gubbins. I think ours contained about three quarters of a bottle of gin; boy it was potent, a truly glorious concoction!

It was definitely understated and, naturally, nobody had any idea that it was possibly strong enough to catapult all the mad hats straight over the balcony and into the Creek in one fell swoop. Without a doubt, there would have been many a thick head the following morning and, without a doubt, it was a humdinger of a party!

Christmas was now looming and plans had to be made. As you know, it really doesn't matter where one is in the world, Christmas has to be celebrated. But how was this going to happen here? I feared an awful lot of ingenuity would be required, but we were getting quite good at this ingenious thing, so maybe the problem wouldn't be so bad after all! Fingers crossed.

Miraculously, parts of the Souk suddenly turned into a tinsel town and one was able to pick up a few bits and pieces, which would add a little sparkle and at least show willing! It was all a little tacky but nevertheless it helped to get the show on the road.

Alas, I didn't think Father Christmas would be appearing with his reindeer in this neck of the woods; now that would be a surprise and a half. I fear the locals would find it hard to recover from the spectacle. On the other hand, if an expatriate wag had reported a sighting of Papa Noel and his reindeer, I'm perfectly sure that Mr Johnnie Walker would have had something to do with it.

A very amusing couple had recently arrived in town, having been posted up from Muscat. We got along like a house on fire and when they suggested that they would 'do Christmas' I couldn't believe my luck. I was going to be spared a monumental headache – or was I – nothing was ever as it seemed!

Now it was all going to be fun; our day was sorted, what a relief. There was always a bit of a bother at this time of the year, but there we were on Christmas morning, looking forward to a very happy day indeed. We were about to set sail for a drinks party and were in high spirits.

We were not alone as we had invited a young army officer to join us for the celebrations, as a gesture of kindness, I might add. I very much feared though that by the end of the day he might have thought otherwise and would rather have been anywhere else than tagging along with us. Hollow legs were definitely required that day!

Such Fun!

Yes, we had woken to another sunny morning in Dubai and it was Christmas Day in 1971, so different from our Christmases of yesteryear but there was no point looking back because we were 'here' and it was 'now'.

Christmas had always been about family and friends and although we had no immediate family with us, neither did anybody else. Consequently, we had morphed into one big happy family and, I think, that was how it should be.

We were ready and raring to go; firstly, to a glorious little drinks party, which should, without a doubt, start the day off with a bang as everybody would be in a party mood.

One had to pinch oneself though to register that it was actually Christmas Day as the temperature was rapidly rising and the relentless sun was beating down. As we now know, that was par for the course in Dubai — wall to wall sunshine, even on Christmas Day! A snowy scene was just a dream!

After consuming some very dodgy cocktails with equally dodgy names, like Bull Shots, Mud in Your Eye and various other outlandish drinks, nobody cared too much where they were, which was possibly just as well!

It sure was different from the partaking of a little dry sherry before Christmas lunch, which would possibly have been the norm for many back home. This was 'let your hair down' time with a vengeance, or was it the devil take the hindmost!

Naturally, we were keeping an eye on the movements of our host and hostess for the evening's celebrations, being prepared to take our cue from them as to when we should depart, as they were there too.

It soon became blatantly obvious that their evening dinner party was very far from their minds at that moment in time, if they had remembered at all that it was even Christmas Day! My goodness, they were having such fun, talk about being full of party spirit! I feared the worst but there was nothing I could do except roll my eyes heavenwards and pray!

We eventually disentangled ourselves from this happy throng imagining that our chums would be following very shortly, as they surely had quite a lot to organize, even if their houseboy was supposedly in charge! We discovered later that was not the case; in fact, they were the last to leave with not a care in the world. We must have been off our heads to have ever thought otherwise.

The three of us returned to base to lick our wounds and recharge our batteries in readiness for the evening's festivities. We surely didn't have too much time. As we were becoming very adept at organizing quick turnarounds, this now presented no problem. Our battle cry had to be, 'Lead on, McDuff!' My goodness, they didn't call us 'team Constabubble' for nothing!

I almost forgot that we had left a turkey quietly cooking in the oven. Oh my God, I hoped it hadn't flown away or been burnt to smithereens — who was brave enough to look? Don't you agree everything always looks so much better if one is wearing a pair of rose coloured spectacles? And this was no exception. On peering into the oven, in my slightly pickled state, I reckoned that the bird was ready and raring to go too, simply cooked to perfection. How clever was that?

It was now 7pm and the designated time for our departure. We set off together with the turkey, which had by now been stuffed, very ungallantly, into a cold box. All four of us made our way along the road to the little bungalow which these chums inhabited at the head of the Creek.

On driving into the parking area, we got the distinct feeling that something definitely wasn't right; the house was in total darkness and all around was deathly quiet. Actually, the place seemed to be totally deserted. They couldn't still be at the drinks party, or could they? Had I got this so terribly wrong and we were not expected after all? Where the hell was everyone, it was like a graveyard. We began to panic. What to do?

Goodness gracious, we ratted on the door but not a sound was to be heard. We wondered where the houseboy was, where our hosts were and where the baby was. Had they all been abducted? Equally as important, there were no glorious cooking smells wafting around; what on earth had happened?

We pondered as to what our next move should be but were bereft of ideas. One good thing was that at least we wouldn't go hungry as the turkey was still trailing along behind us.

With that, the houseboy came flying around the corner of the bungalow, totally agitated and virtually incoherent but the gist of it was that Sahib, Memsahib and the baby were all sleeping — I think they must have passed out, well not the baby, of course. What to do, he wailed. It would obviously take a bucket of cold water to resurrect them and he couldn't do anything about dinner either because there were no potatoes in the house!

The latter problem was easily remedied as he was swiftly despatched to the Souk to buy said potatoes, whilst we stood there not knowing whether to laugh or cry, terrified that our trump card – which was the turkey – would abscond too.

I am sure there has got to be a moral to this story and that is to get everything organized before you let yourself in for a long drinks session on Christmas morning. Mind you, I'm now sounding like Miss Goody Two-Shoes, and that will never do as, in fact, it's all these little cameos that go a long way to making special celebrations so much more fun and memorable.

Yes, it's being caught up in situations like that one that are so ridiculous you find yourself falling about laughing! My goodness, this would never happen in leafy Surrey, would it?

After a while, our sheepish hosts appeared minutes before they were about to be drenched with a bucket of water although, I might add, looking somewhat the worse for wear.

By this time, the houseboy had returned from the Souk with the potatoes, the champagne had been opened and hey presto we were once again off on the road to ruin. By now we had smiles on our faces as at last all was well, and we were back on track with a resounding toot and a hoot! I'm not too sure if we ever noticed whether we were eating turkey or flying pigeon, or even cared!

I can honestly say that that Christmas Day in Dubai had been like no other we had ever experienced in our lives. Was it good or was it bad, and did we miss the folks back home?

On reflection, I think I can safely say we had all done a jolly good job at helping Dubai don her Christmas hat, pull a cracker or two along the way and generally let her hair down. I suspect, though, it was from that moment on that our Christmases, as we had known them, were never quite the same again!

What a day that was! I hope you have been amused.

New Year's Eve – 1971!

How we ever survived that Christmas Day I will never know. Although, I would go as far as to say that our stamina together with the fortitude of our host and hostess should surely have made us good candidates for the Carry On Regardless awards!

What the hell, it was 1971 and we were living in a country that didn't even recognize the very existence of Christmas. Why was it then that, collectively, we were hell-bent on running amuck. At every opportunity we seemed to be doing our damnedest to let the locals know that they would really, really be missing out if they hadn't sighted Father Christmas somewhere around town by Christmas Eve — preferably trying to squeeze through their air con ducts.

At the rate we were going we were well on our way to giving the locals a collective chip on their shoulders or land up in the clink; the latter more likely!

It was so much fun! Christmas Day was our only day off and, consequently, it was back to work on the 26th, nursing monumental thick heads. But we were all made of strong stuff, weren't we? No slackers were allowed in this neck of the woods or, as the saying goes, this side of the next sand dune!

We knew the next few days would sort out the men from the boys as work didn't stop and the parties continued. We also had to bear in mind that we were on countdown for the biggest one of all — New Year's Eve! Golly gosh, soldier on we must!

Wonders will never cease — we realized that we just might have made our mark when an invitation to the one and only New Year's Eve party that everyone wished to be invited to plonked through our proverbial letter box.

Oh what joy, we had been invited to George's famous Fancy Dress Barge Party, which was held annually on a barge that was, naturally, moored somewhere up the Creek. The receipt of this invitation confirmed it all; yes, we were gradually rising up that slippery greasy poll called the social ladder.

On reflection, it's very strange to think that receiving an invitation to a specific party should assume such great importance but, alas, these are the vagaries of the human race. We all want to be those special people, the movers and shakers without whom no party is complete. That was even true in this relatively unknown desert township; God knows what it must be like in a place known to have a little more social cachet.

Naturally, our fancy dress attire had to wow but, thank goodness, our mad Christmas Day chums were on the invitation list too; what a bonus. If they could rescue Christmas dinner whilst sleeping off the excesses of lunchtime drinks with no potatoes in the house to boot, then surely they could be relied upon to conjure up a plan pretty smartly.

I was not wrong and it was unanimously decided that the four of us would go as the Three Blind Mice and the Farmer's Wife, thought up in a thrice; what a great idea!

In the cold light of day it was really obvious that three of us would go as mice wearing black dishdashas, bright pink floppy ears with pink tails to match, and the Farmer's Wife would be wearing a white dishdasha and would be wielding a big knife. All went according to plan and, in fact, we won a prize.

I must say it was quite an experience, not only locating the barge but then clambering aboard along a rickety gangplank, but that was all part of the fun.

We then rocked and rolled the night away including the barge, which seemed to be listing from port to starboard rather frequently and, at times, we had the distinct feeling that she just might not stay the course and die the death with us scrambling towards the shore. Thank goodness these worries were unfounded!

Midnight was heralded in with the hooting of ships' sirens. These ships were moored up and down the Creek and were eerily silhouetted by the twinkling lights that were dancing around, playing ducks and drakes over the water, creating a veritable kaleidoscope of colour.

In the distance one could just make out the outline of a mosque in Bur Dubai, which seemed to be presiding majestically over the proceedings. It was truly awesome.

We were as far away from Big Ben as it was possible to be, in such a different world but, in its fashion, quite magical, and a place which had kindly offered us its hand of friendship — one which we had gladly accepted.

Yes, I think it's safe to say that at that moment we realized we were in a place we really regarded as home. Our new address was most definitely Creekside, Dubai, and that's where we could be found.

After our riotous New Year's Eve party, we felt sure that 1972 would definitely shape up to be a fantastic year. After all, we were now part of the very fabric that made up this tiny expatriate community and we had, I think, earned our spurs.

How? Well, by never falling by the wayside over the past year, at least almost never, and we were always game for a laugh. Attributes that were definitely required to become a paid-up member of this, dare I say it, Exclusive Club!

Okay, we had welcomed in the New Year with a bang, a hoot and a wail. What do I mean? Well, loud bangs from fireworks thundering up and over the Creek, which were accompanied by our collective oohs and aahs, as if we hadn't seen fireworks before! We had the illuminations but no accompanying 'son et lumière'.

Unfortunately, the 1812 Overture thundering out over the Creek would, I most definitely think, have terrified the locals and sent them into a collective frenzy, possibly thinking a coup was imminent! By this time the ships' hooters were competing for attention and then, not to be outdone, the mullahs joined in; what a racket.

If one's head hadn't already succumbed to all those potent cocktails, then this little cacophony would surely do the trick quite nicely. Where were the Alka-Seltzers?

We had given 1971 a right royal send-off and now we had to somehow be bright-eyed and bushy-tailed to herald in the first day of 1972, which in fine tradition was to be inaugurated by a party; what a surprise! You didn't expect me to say that!

Rent-a-crowd had been mustered and was required to be at a villa just off the beach road in Jumeirah for a lunchtime Black Velvet party – that's champagne and Guinness to you and me – but, after the night before, it was just one terrible alcoholic concoction too many for little old me. At this rate all the pharmacists in town would surely have sold out of Alka-Seltzers by nightfall.

A little snapshot of how we managed to continue to keep the camp fires burning, as it were. Actually, it wasn't too difficult, and we definitely proved that it was really quite easy to spread a lot of fun and an equal amount of happiness and cheer around and about with a little help from the Liquor Store, the best shop in town! Cheers, Mr G.M. — wishing you a Happy New Year too!

It was inevitable that at some stage over the Christmas season most of us would feel somewhat stranded and, perhaps, a little homesick in this small desert kingdom where we had unwittingly found ourselves.

This was especially true when repeatedly hearing nostalgic songs like 'I'll Be Home for Christmas' by was it Bing Crosby or maybe Frank Sinatra, knowing that even if it was your greatest wish it surely was an impossible dream.

On reflection, Dubai came up trumps. Uncannily, she knew just how we might be feeling and because of that she made sure all our festivities went with a bang and come what may we would enjoy an epic few days, the likes of which would be unforgettable.

We knew then that there was only one place in the whole wide world where we would, in future, like to celebrate Christmas and herald in the New Year and that was, and I expect still is, Dubai. You definitely brought a smile to our faces, thank you!

Best Foot Forward!

After the shenanigans of the past two weeks, I had decided that I never wanted to go to another party, drink another dodgy cocktail or wake up after only having had a few hours' sleep, more than likely nursing a thumping head.

That was all too much to have to contend with, let alone knowing that this merry-go-round would be starting all over again in a few hours' time; we should be so popular! Stop the world, I want to get off; just for a moment, please!

That, my friends, admirably sums up 24 hours in Dubai during the silly season. Lest we forget, and would you believe, somewhere in that time span one had to clear the decks for a few hours for another funny pastime, called work! Actually, it definitely wasn't 'get me to the church on time' it was more like 'get me to the office on time', preferably compos mentis!

Yes, we had survived not only all those parties but, most importantly, 1971. How would I rate our progress? To purloin a phrase from those dreaded school reports, good steady progress had been made but needed a little more dedication and attention to detail!

In other words, we were no longer just hanging on in there, clutching at any flotsam and jetsam that flowed by. No, I am very relieved to report that we were swimming along nicely and would go as far as to say gathering a little momentum along the way. At least we had not sunk without trace!

Arousing from my slumber that first workday morning in 1972, I had a little time to contemplate and wonder what the new year would have in store. How many surprises would it have up its sleeve, good or bad? More importantly, would I be up for the challenge? Don't be silly, of course, I would!

In those days there was always a buzz in the air; in fact, life was for living and it would seem that there was no better place in the world to illustrate this point than Dubai.

Leafy, sleepy Surrey was now light years away, her memory fading fast. This was coupled with the memory of that other girl wearing pearls, the one who boarded that plane for pastures new in fear and trepidation but, as the song goes, 'Just look at her now'! My, what a transformation!

It was now time to shake a leg and start the new year with my best foot forward; I was off, are you coming?

I had no doubt that Mike would be very busy with his Bitumen Supply Company, as they were opening bitumen depots up and down the Gulf.

He would also be making sure that his little tankers were operating up to speed, ensuring that there was a constant supply of bitumen making its way down from Abadan to meet the requirements of the construction companies, who were busy building the infrastructure.

Those desert tracks were being tamed, morphing rapidly into spanking new highways. In some cases, dual carriageways were on the agenda; wow, that would indeed be progress. Naturally, we were blissfully unaware that those first major construction works were the very foundations on which today's Dubai has so successfully been crafted.

Once these initial projects were completed, desert bashing would surely become a thing of the past, only being enjoyed by the daredevils amongst us and called 'Friday fun', now not having to be endured out of necessity. Maybe the next pastime would be doing a ton up the new Abu Dhabi highway but that exercise wouldn't be without its dangers too. Why? Because the road was scheduled to cut across the local camels' domain.

Camels were always to be seen trotting hither and yon in the desert, not surprisingly; after all, it was their neck of the woods. What was going to happen once the highway was complete and they realized that this extraordinary man-made object, which had appeared in their midst, would most definitely hamper their movements. I wonder who would have right of way?

At present, they were free spirits, with no constraints, wandering contentedly to pastures new to their hearts' content. Imagine what a terrifying experience it would be sighting one of these big beasts of the desert galloping towards you when you were driving at a rate of knots up the new highway. It definitely wouldn't be a sight for sore eyes, it would be an encounter of nightmare proportions, to be avoided at all costs!

I too would be busy, waltzing around the airport with a smile on my face and surely not a care in the world, possibly whistling a happy tune. Sometimes though, life has to be taken a little more seriously. As this was the new year, it was the time when sons and daughters of expatriates working in Dubai had to return to school in the UK, or maybe elsewhere in the world.

This was a heart wrenching time for many a family, especially those with young children. In those days, boys of eight or nine years old were required to be schooled back home, as there was no adequate schooling beyond that age in Dubai.

As the expatriate community was so small, we mostly knew each other. I can vividly remember one distraught mother phoning me with a heartfelt plea, which was to say that her son was so very distressed about returning to school but could possibly be persuaded to board the plane if I personally accompanied him — now that surely was an honour indeed!

It really was a stomach wrenching time standing at check-in seeing distraught mothers beside their equally distraught offspring, with a father a few steps behind trying to make light of the occasion but with enormous difficulty. All knowing in their hearts that this shouldn't be happening and if it hadn't been for fate playing a hand they too, like

148

me, would have been tucked up in Surrey or somewhere similar within walking distance of a school — oh, the injustice of it all.

Time marched on and a BOAC VC10 waited for no one. What a tearful handover it was with everyone crying and me trying to be all things to all people without dissolving into tears too. At last, clutching the hands of the little ones, and with no looking back, we whizzed into the departure lounge and usually managed to time it so there was no hanging around.

To board the plane, one had to descend one floor via what we used to call a whirligig, which was actually designed like a fairground helter-skelter. It was a unique design, way ahead of its time, and the architects Page and Broughton were indeed commended for dreaming up such a gateway — but was it a gateway to heaven or to hell? I think for these little souls it must have been like descending down a whirligig to hell!

My mission was almost complete once we had climbed those steep steps and I had handed my charges over to the onward going stewardess with a wink and a nod. Although I did have one very important last task, and that was to settle them in, make sure that their seat belts were fastened and that they were as comfortable as possible. In return, I usually received a big soggy kiss.

With that I would assure them that the Easter holidays would be here before they knew it and, guess what, I would definitely be on the tarmac to greet them on their arrival. That usually brought a watery smile.

On that sad note my next task was to seek out their parents. That was easy — they were always to be found on the upper deck of the departure lounge waving their little ones off, as the big blue bird was getting ready for take-off. They almost always had tears streaming down their faces — it was so very sad.

This was what being part of the Dubai community was all about and the motto must have been 'all for one and one for all'. Yes, we needed each other for better or worse!

The sad tears were wiped away as, somehow, life had to go on, and Easter wasn't too far away, was it? Then it would be the return of those little heroes, who would no doubt be ten feet taller, possibly sporting a new front tooth together with a wonky smile, and maybe in need of a haircut too. This time though there would only be tears of joy.

Ground hostess, Dubai International Airport
British Overseas Airways Corporation

Brainwave!

I was still recovering from my first real test as a ground hostess at the airport. Did I pass muster? Indeed I hoped so. What a harrowing experience for everyone involved, but I was so very glad that I was able to assist, in my own little way, and maybe make those dreaded goodbyes a little easier to bear.

Actually, on those occasions, I think I morphed into a real life Mary Poppins in my endeavours to jolly everyone along; maybe I had missed my vocation! Mind you, I would definitely have needed to take singing lessons! Whatever, if I could help in any way to ease those anxious moments, then that was what I must do.

With all the boarders dispatched the airport returned to normal, which meant being exceedingly quiet. Actually, most mornings, I virtually had the place to myself; my goodness, what a wonderful skittle alley the main concourse would have made!

I was able to wander around to my heart's content, like a kid in a candy shop, exploring every nook and cranny, upstairs, downstairs and in the lady's chamber! I occasionally found myself in the basement, where the kitchens could be found, passing the time of day with the catering staff.

They too were often at a loose end because very few of the airlines passing through habitually utilized their services. Maybe they had horrors of old goat being on the menu, I jest!

I know, it really is quite unimaginable knowing the frantic pace of today's Dubai that there was ever a time when the airport wasn't inundated with planes and people 24/7.

It really must sound like the Stone Age to you but, back then, there were days which were bereft of any international arrivals or departures whatsoever, amazing!

This is a snapshot of how today's world-beating Dubai International Airport took its first tentative steps into the 'big time' and just look at her now, that is called progress! Those were the days when one had to wait maybe one or two days for a plane to take you to London or Bombay. How times have changed! Woe betide anybody if they couldn't keep up. In retrospect, a fast pair of running shoes were required, possibly jet propelled!

The home front had settled down too. Sailing had taken a back seat as it was deemed a little too cold to potter up and down the Creek in next to nothing. In fact, my time was being taken up by weightier things. Like what? I can hear you ask.

Would you believe, I was now a very important person; well, I thought I was and that was all that mattered! I had been elected onto the Social Committee of the Country Club. Alas, I wasn't too sure how much my input would help to make it a fine dining experience for the members. I was always brimming over with ideas but most of them were somewhat crackpot, to say the least. Once again, I think it was three out of ten, must try harder!

We held our first committee meeting in the new year when it was decided that the inaugural function should be a little do scheduled towards the end of January. This didn't really leave too much time for a brainwave to occur and what we really needed was divine inspiration, but where was that going to come from? Actually, the solution was staring us in the face all the time and, not surprisingly, we were just a little slow off the mark!

So many of the expats in Dubai were Scottish or claimed to be and, for some reason best known to themselves, they all had the same great friend called Johnnie Walker! Everybody seemed to know this chap and his popularity knew no bounds! In fact, knowing him would seem to entitle most able-bodied expats in Dubai to be eligible to join the Caledonian Society too! Now there was a thing!

After much dilly-dallying we had, what is it called, a light bulb moment or brainwave, whatever. How about holding our version of a Burns Supper? This would engage the Scots in our midst and also be a good starting point for the first ever hooley at the Country Club, history in the making for sure!

Having unanimously decided on this splendid idea we sprang into action. First things first, we had to find paper and a pencil to start a list. Why is it that to do anything bloody lists are required? But bloody lists we had to have, one for this and one for that and one for everything else!

I might add that most of these bits of paper had nothing on them because ideas were thin on the ground. In our exuberance, we had not given a thought to the fact that, as yet, there were no real kitchen facilities, serving areas, plates, glasses and cutlery; in fact, the place was bare!

Undaunted, an idea sprung to mind. I now knew many of the military who had been posted to Sharjah, either serving in the TOS or the RAF and also there were small contingents of 'an.others' dotted around. To cut a long story short, a chef together with a sidekick and even a lone piper were press-ganged into action. How amazing was that?

These boys had been volunteered to come to a maiden's rescue by my military chums, who to this day shall remain nameless. Unfortunately, these poor guys didn't know what they were being volunteered for, most definitely Army manoeuvres with a difference! Obviously top secret too!

In the end, we had to leave it to the Cookhouse Boys to conjure up some delicious eats; after all, beggars can't be choosers. We just hoped and prayed that this food was not actually earmarked for the Officers' Mess! What the hell, we were surely on a roll!

We thought we were so smart being such great organizers, which really meant seeing just how much we could get away with by using feminine guile. Well, how did it all turn out? They say pride comes before a fall, don't they?

As it was supposed to be a Burns Supper we really should have had haggis on the menu but that was definitely out of the question. Actually,

I don't think the menu contained one ingredient normally associated with a traditional Burns Supper except, of course, a wee dram or two! That would more than suffice though!

With great anticipation, we assembled together to organize what we could in readiness for the arrival of the cavalry, this being in the form of a commandeered Army Bedford truck, which would hopefully contain all the victuals required to make the evening go with a bang.

The guests were beginning to arrive and clogging up the bar, eagerly waiting for what they were sure would be a sumptuous feast, especially as we were not actually doing the cooking — where was their faith?

The first person from Sharjah to arrive was the lone piper. Jock took up his place beside the tree on the mound at the top of the hill and beneath the light of the silvery moon proceeded to play those wonderful laments that always bring a tear to the eye, and this evening was no exception. Yes, Scots can get a little maudlin listening to the skirl of the pipes when far away from home! It's par for the course!

Time seemed to be racing by with no sign of the Bedford truck which was carrying all the victuals. Oh my God, where was it? What had happened? We waited and waited but by now all the partygoers were either pickled or fractious, and we were becoming exceedingly anxious. It had seemed like a good idea at the time. Surely the British Army couldn't and wouldn't let us down, would they? What could we do? Nothing really, we had no means of communication, not even carrier pigeons fly at night!

Much later, by which time everybody was past caring and threatening to sack the Social Committee, an Army Scout car was seen dashing up the Al Awir Road towards the clubhouse bringing the most astonishing news – which you will never guess – and that was there had been an attempted coup in Sharjah.

The Sheik had been killed together with one of his guards and all hell had been let loose. The palace had been surrounded by Sharjah soldiers and troops from the TOS. In the ensuing skirmish several troops had been wounded together with a British captain. Thank goodness though, the rebels surrendered the following morning.

To this day, I'm not too sure whether we ever received the food, if it fell by the wayside or possibly was shot to smithereens. One thing was certain though, none of us would ever forget that night in a hurry. Yes, the first major function at Dubai Country Club surely went with a very unexpected bang!

And still the piper played on, bewitching us with his mournful tunes and reminding us that we were not marking the Battle of Bannockburn but a battle much closer to home. This battle was taking place right under our noses, up the road in Sharjah, and some might say a little too close for comfort.

Bull Shots!

My God, who would have thought that a nice little social gathering to mark the very being of Dubai Country Club could have ended in such mayhem?

That evening will be remembered for its very unexpected outcome and before you jump to the wrong conclusions, no, it wasn't that we were all possibly rolling in the aisles, nothing of the sort! It was because the very peaceful existence that we generally enjoyed in those parts had unexpectedly been shattered! My goodness, whatever next!

Needless to say, we were all eager to know what on earth was happening up in Sharjah but back in that Stone Age we had no means of communication, let alone instant communication.

Consequently, discovering just what had gone on or maybe was still going on, to render us all agog and most definitely all of a twitter, would have to wait until the morning. Then without a doubt the jungle drums would most definitely be beating all the way to downtown Dubai.

Thank goodness though, we didn't have to wait too long before news reached our twitching ears, which was that a force of 18 armed supporters of the former ruler of Sharjah – with him, no less, leading the raiding party – besieged the palace and, in the process, managed to kill the then ruler, causing considerable mayhem whilst they were about it.

Reinforcements arrived in the form of the Union Defence Force, the renamed Trucial Oman Scouts, who had been summoned to quell the fighting. In so doing, they unfortunately sustained numerous casualties.

One of these was a young British officer, who naturally became the hero of the whole escapade and the talk of the town. Oh, what a to-do it all was. From our standpoint, though, it was all rather exciting. Whatever next, we asked ourselves!

We were soon receiving blow by blow accounts, straight from the horse's mouth, because the British officer just happened to be a chum. As he needed rest and recuperation there was no better place to take tea together with something a little stronger than our abode. Incidentally, this was where the best afternoon tea and cocktails were served this side of the Ritz!

Oh, what fun it was turning out to be! We were regaled with the story of just how the coup was dealt with – naturally, swiftly and efficiently – and marvelled at the bravery of our officer chum. Actually, it was a little like a real live episode of 'Dan Dare rides again'!

So in our way we had a little walk-on part in this drama, something like being mentioned in dispatches if you know what I mean. At least it kept the story reverberating around for a little longer and, at times, turned our apartment into something akin to the Downtown Officers' Mess, an exclusive club, if ever there was one!

Talking about officers, there seemed to be a gradual influx of various military types appearing on the scene as a Military Advisory Team was deployed to Sharjah. Then there was the gradual formation of the Dubai Defence Force which, in the first instance, was headed up by British officers and, if that wasn't sufficient, there were a few other military and naval wallahs wafting around and about. Dubai was being turned upside down.

These chaps soon made their mark one way and another and boy did they like to party. We thought we knew a thing or two about raving it up but we were in for a big surprise together with lots of fun. They nearly always had a trick or two up their sleeves, some more outrageous than others!

I can recall two chums, one a naval chap and the other, I think, was the military attaché, who delighted in giving lethal little drinks parties where they served Bloody Marys and another great little number called a Bull Shot. The latter, I think, originated in the Navy.

This consisted of a mixture of consommé and vodka, I would wager more vodka than consommé. Never having heard of this particular cocktail, let alone downed one, we all thought they were fantastic and naturally the height of sophistication.

Actually, in our naivety we imagined that we were sipping cold soup, which was very welcome on such a hot day, thinking to ourselves how very thoughtful our hosts were and, needless to say, being totally oblivious as to their potency. Oh how we were hoodwinked!

In turn, these two delighted in watching us down I don't know how many in quick succession; in fact, we were downing them, or maybe drowning in them, as fast as they could be made, having no idea of the consequences. Yes, you have guessed, we learnt the hard way!

It was a good job these little parties weren't held on board a ship because I'm sure we would have all fallen overboard. On reflection, maybe that's why we never saw the pair in charge of a ship, it was too darn dangerous. They were lethal on dry land so goodness knows what they would have been like at sea, no doubt rocking and rolling all over the place.

Their parties were such fun we forgave them anything and always hoped that we would be heading up their next guest list but not before we had acquired some hollow legs.

At about that time, the Dubai Defence Force was gradually taking shape with British officers being seconded to help the start-up. We met one officer and his wife, literally not long after they had landed at the airport. They were a delightful couple who hit the town running and actually never stopped until they left many, many years later.

They arrived out of the blue and were welcomed with open arms. They must have landed on a Thursday evening and were immediately whisked by their greeter to the Sahara Nightclub, where we could usually be found boogying the night away. Introductions were made and I can honestly say that from that moment on none of us looked back and I don't think our feet ever touched the ground again.

Why was that? Because every day was deemed to be a party day with these two around! We did not know it at the time, but we had just been introduced to our team leader and from then on we were going to be kept on our toes, in more ways than one. The catchphrase from that moment on was 'Golly gosh'!

Am I beginning to give you the impression that Dubai was fast turning into the party capital of the world? Well, that may have been correct but we had to try and remember that we also had work to do and that we shouldn't complain when it interfered with our ever burgeoning social life!

I also had another pressing problem. As the golf course was now operational, the ladies – yes, I mean those ladies who played golf and incidentally were usually a dab hand at that dreaded card game of bridge – were gathering in the wings, or I should say sand dunes, and I was expected to join them, oh dear!

They were determined to give the gentlemen a run for their money, their mantra being 'if you can't beat them, join them'! The chaps, on occasions, looked quietly bemused when this small but formidable army of very determined ladies descended on the first tee to begin their game. The gauntlet was thrown down. 'Let battle commence,' was the cry!

Where did I fit in? Well, I knew the rudiments of golf having had many a lesson in my youth, so I too was expected to become a member of this glorious 'barmy army' of formidable golfing ladies! They did slightly terrify me, though!

To this end, I needed some clubs and also a few lessons, not only on perfecting my swing but on how to survive trudging around this giant sandpit – which was now lovingly called a golf course – without falling by the wayside with exhaustion. I was always puzzled. Was it actually meant to be fun or an endurance test? I could never figure that one out!

After acquiring clubs, the next priority was to arm myself with a piece of AstroTurf from which one was able to play the next ball after if it fell onto the marked fairway. This was called a preferred lie or, if wished, you could make a little mound of sand just beside where the ball lay and place the ball on top, which enabled you to strike it more cleanly.

It was all very crafty really and the irony was that, on paper, the whole operation seemed a little crackpot but once one got the hang of things the course played almost like a dream. Even the browns, which were made by oiling the sand and rolling it flat, played quite true. It was

159

quite astonishing — the ingenuity of man knows no bounds, or where there's a will there's a way.

I got my act together and usually played once a week on Ladies' Day, extremely badly, I might add! If I'm honest, I found it hard work trudging around. It was usually very hot and, oh dear, my lady golfing companions were all so competitive — it makes me feel exhausted thinking about it.

Frequently, I would think longingly of 'Buttercup' my sailing boat and wish I was pitting my wits against the elements rather than limping around this very hot sandy desert, now referred to lovingly as a golf course, chasing a little red golf ball to boot.

On reflection, I am very sad that my stoicism was never acknowledged and rewarded with the tiniest of medals, wouldn't you agree?

Deep End!

We survived the coup in Sharjah, unlike the poor old Sheik — what an ignominious ending he had! I suppose, if I'm honest, we managed to garner a lot of mileage out of all the fun and games that made up the aftermath of this debacle!

My everlasting memory of that night is of the 'lone piper' standing on the hill at the Country Club, piping his head off, whilst we were going round like headless chickens wondering why the posse transporting the food from Sharjah had not arrived.

We were definitely not paying attention to or appreciating those wonderful doleful Scottish laments or indeed attempting a desert version of the Highland fling. Sadly, we were too busy with our own laments!

Life gradually returned to normal; actually, I'm not too sure what constituted as normal in those chaotic days. Our invalided captain was eventually able to return to light duties and, consequently, the apartment was vacated and the Deira Outpost of the TOS Officers' Mess returned from whence it came. I was then able to potter down to the sailing club most afternoons and Mike was back enjoying his golf.

If you have been following my story, you will have noted that I have only once mentioned another pastime happily played in so many drawing rooms, which is that illustrious game of cards called bridge. Enjoyed by many, I hasten to mention it's a card game that is definitely not for the faint-hearted and obviously this is the reason why it has only received a fleeting mention in my musings!

I had obviously been lulled into a false sense of security as once again I was about to be wrong-footed. The phone rang, always quite a novelty in this neck of the woods, and as we all know curiosity usually has a devastating effect on the cat and this call was to be no exception.

Unbeknown to me, I was about to receive my second fateful invitation – or was it a command – which involved a pack of playing cards. Could I please make up a fourth for bridge; my goodness, they must have been desperate! I was too slow, fell straight in at the deep end and there was nothing much I could do about it. So there I was ensnared once again.

Foolishly I thought that after the last epic occasion when I was gaily trumping my partner's trumps that the whole of Dubai would have steered clear. My, oh my, they must have thrown caution to the wind or indeed have very short memories.

They say variety is the spice of life but I could really have done without any more 'spice in my life'. Actually, I had been congratulating myself as to how well I had recovered from all the recent excitement then this happened. It would definitely put years on me!

Why couldn't I be like 'normal women' who usually liked nothing better than participating in genteel drawing room activities, such as gossiping over a leisurely coffee, often quietly bragging about how many invitations to various functions they had received lately. This was a not so subtle way of announcing to the assembled ladies as to just what a popular couple you were. This little act was normally calculated to make your very best friends green with envy especially if their tally wasn't somewhat similar. Once that was achieved you knew your morning had been a success!

Obviously, your brinkmanship didn't stop there, your children always seemed to be doing so much better than everyone else's and it goes without saying that your cook/houseboy was simply outstanding and you hadn't had to teach him anything at all; yes, a paragon, he could even make a soufflé, no doubt blindfolded, such a clever boy.

On these dreaded occasions it was quite normal for the majority of the coterie to be struck dumb for fear of putting their pretty feet well and truly in it, as there was nothing worse than feeling that you might be letting the preferable side down! Heaven forbid!

After about an hour of this chatter-rooing, I was normally ready to bolt but was trapped. One had to play by the rules otherwise another black mark would be winging its way onto your report sheet to be circulated around and about whilst your back was turned.

It goes without saying that the majority of these drawing room ladies played bridge too as they normally didn't embark on anything too physical, other than wagging their tongues. My goodness though, for this sport most of them would have been in line for a gold medal.

Luckily there were demarcation lines so normally our paths didn't cross and, consequently, we managed to rub along nicely, gingerly sidestepping one another. This was a well-tried practice, from time immemorial, which suited all parties until, yes, there was a desperate need for a fourth for bridge, then all those rules and all that caution was deftly thrown to the wind. If you were really, really unlucky you would be caught in the slipstream and that would be that.

What I hadn't altogether realized was that to be deemed a drawing room lady par excellence, in that day and age, necessitated being a dab hand at shuffling those dreaded cards. Gone were the days when you were expected to sit bolt upright in an uncomfortable chair with your legs neatly crossed, squinting at your petit point, trying oh so hard not to stab yourself with the needle, thus ruining your exquisite embroidery.

It goes without saying that I was still no further forward with the comprehension of the dreaded conventions and rules without which the game of bridge would not exist. Actually, something told me that I was not too bothered but I had better keep that to myself, otherwise a few more black marks would be lobbed my way.

I was now ready for the off, fussing over my dress – was it alright, would I pass muster – after all, I really must have a little something in my favour as it would quickly become apparent that I was devoid of any card playing skills! I was now ready for the off!

I arrived on time to be greeted by the houseboy who walked me through to where the ladies were already waiting for me, the dreaded fourth! We exchanged pleasantries and cut for partners — no hanging around there!

Oh, yes, once again I was asked what convention I played. I really felt that this time I shouldn't say the Chopin as it wasn't deemed to be too funny on my previous exposure into the lion's den; consequently, this time, I replied, 'Any one you prefer. I'm very versatile and always like to oblige!' With no further ado the cards were shuffled and dealt and once I had them in my sticky paws I knew I was undoubtedly heading for an afternoon of sheer purgatory and these poor ladies were going to have to endure a very unexpected and trying afternoon too, attempting to decipher my calls. Yes, they would have quickly realized that they had in their midst the bridge player from hell.

Delightful Company!

We were enjoying happy days. We had time to relax and enjoy our surroundings; yes, Dubai was now very much home and surprise, surprise we couldn't really imagine living anywhere else. Did I need a doctor urgently? Maybe I was suffering from a severe attack of the noonday sun? Surely it was anybody's guess!

Without registering what was happening, we were morphing into little Arabs or, put in a different parlance, seasoned expats. There was one thing we had failed to take into account — that it just might be extremely difficult for us to happily step back into our old Surrey boots! What to do?

Actually, that was possibly a good thing because we then wouldn't have known whether we were coming or going. I'm sure we would have been so fussed about all the 'what ifs' that, no doubt, we would not have enjoyed the moment, let alone being in awe of the gentle unfolding of our magical mystery journey.

Whatever next! Out of the blue, astonishing news was received from London. Harold Wilson, the then British Labour Prime Minister had decided, with a grand flourish no less, to withdraw all British troops east of Suez and, in fact, the actual funding thereof.

As any sane person would understand, this edict threw the entire region into a collective tiswas. 'How do we overcome this?' was the cry. It was of particular concern as the area had, for so many years, been a British protectorate. Effectively, Wilson was pulling the plug and seemingly not giving thought to the long-standing relationship which the British Government and the Gulf States enjoyed. At the stroke of a pen the security of the entire region was put into jeopardy. It was blindingly obvious that a solution had to be found rather smartly. I will attempt to explain how the problem was overcome; it's an interesting little meander into the history books.

As can only be expected after such an edict, difficult times were experienced by some and there were opportunities for others. The Trucial Oman Scouts would need to be reorientated and would be renamed the Union Defence Force. RAF Sharjah would be taking its leave after many, many years of swooping over this territory, checking for marauders and pirates on the high seas.

When they were not flying and had some free time they occasionally joined us for picnics at Al Hamriya or Ajman and always took great delight in frightening the living daylights out of those of us who loved to swim and ski in the balmy waters of the Gulf.

They would tell us, with huge grins on their faces, that there were always big mouthed sharks basking in the shallow waters, waiting patiently for an opportunity to get their giant teeth into a tasty bit of flesh — our flesh. Mostly, we chose not to listen; it sure was an incentive, though, to stay upright whilst water skiing! We must have been mad!

If we weren't sidestepping sharks in the Gulf, we could possibly be found sipping cocktails at the British Consulate. Part of their brief was to give parties in order to introduce visiting businessmen and any other official wallahs who may be in town to the local community. We were obviously invited along for our scintillating wit!

Those were heady days, particularly when, in return, we were scooped up and invited to reciprocal bashes maybe on board visiting Royal Navy vessels or up to Sharjah, either with the RAF or at small military units around and about. These soirées were sometimes held at desert encampments, not sophisticated venues and, on occasions, we felt as if we were following in the footsteps of Lawrence of Arabia; it was all rather jolly really!

I digress; I was wandering around the desert in a daydream when I was really heading for Port Rashid as we had been invited to a cocktail party on board a visiting naval vessel. These were always sought after invitations — there is something very romantic about being piped on board a ship, which is dressed overall, to be greeted by the captain who is accompanied by a young officer, both dressed in tropical whites.

This kit could transform even the dullest of chaps, making them look dashing and handsome. Our men would be attired in Gulf rig, which consisted of dress trousers, a white open-necked short sleeved shirt and a cummerbund. As usual, us girls were usually wearing long evening dresses — nothing new there!

These little soirées were so very enjoyable as they were obviously not the norm, and our hosts were naturally attentive and charming. Gentle flirting was the order of the day and if, by chance, there was a lone wife floating around she would be very much in demand; it was quite amazing what that did for the jolly old ego!

It wasn't, 'Would you like to see my etchings?' Oh no, but 'I would love to show you around the wardroom'. It still brings a smile to think how innocent we all were but what fun it all was!

Normally, we girls were given the wink that if the ship was in dock for a few days it was up to us to reciprocate and invite one or two of these chaps to dinner. Now if you have never, as a hostess, had the pleasure of opening your door to receive your dinner guests, who just might happen to be two or three young naval officers once again dressed in their tropical kit, I would say you have definitely been missing a trick or two. I will now change the subject!

And then there were the cocktail parties given by the military, who at that stage were mostly stationed in Sharjah. These were the new boys who were going to fill the gap, or gaps, that would appear when the masses were repatriated.

I would mention that most of the new contingent was being funded, well, in Dubai, by Sheik Rashid. The very last thing he wanted was for the British to withdraw, thus creating a very unhealthy vacuum in that neck of the woods, or I should say sand dunes!

One such party was given by a delightful Scottish colonel and his wife and, if my memory serves me correctly, it was held in a large tent somewhere off the beaten track in Sharjah. Yes, in amongst the sand dunes, what a surprise!

We were once again dressed up to the nines; we learnt at a very early stage that one must never let the side down! Looking back it now seems quite bizarre that it should have been the norm to be so formally attired whilst trotting around the bloody desert.

This party was being held in order for the colonel of this particular advisory team to become acquainted with us, the local movers and shakers, otherwise known as rent-a-crowd!

Word had obviously got about that no party would be complete without our presence and also for the new military arrivals to be reassured that there was more to the desert than camels! I'm sure once orientated they would do their level best to keep this part of the world on an even keel, whilst lending a helping hand to make subsequent parties go with an even bigger swing!

That particular evening we were introduced to yet another half colonel, as they were affectionately nicknamed, and his wife, who were quite delightful. They had just been parachuted in from God knows where and were wondering what the lie of the land was. It was not surprising that they were somewhat apprehensive as since their arrival they had been knee-deep in sand and more bloody sand.

They were frightfully formal and I think the wife was wearing a white mink coat in the middle of the desert – yes, in the middle of the desert – now that's how to cut a dash! Even if you might have been fainting with the heat! I was mesmerized!

Suffice to say, we decided that they needed to be introduced to the local nightlife, so we guided them down the subka track to Dubai and to the famous Bustan Hotel!

It didn't take long to discover that these two were party goers 'par excellence' and that one should not be fooled when meeting military personnel for the first time because they would surely be on their guard. After downing a few gin and tonics, though, caution was usually thrown to the wind and the cry was usually, 'Let the party begin'. Tonight there was another cry of, 'What on earth possessed me to wear this bloody mink coat!' Guess what? It was never seen again!

Going into Bat!

The old jalopy and I were swinging along with our usual gay abandon, merrily hooting and tooting our way around town. If we were not going here or there, then we were definitely going somewhere else!

In retrospect, it was all rather funny, sort of game for a laugh. Actually, it transpired that it was no laughing matter and I quickly realized that I didn't know it all and would have to get to grips with things rather smartly!

It was one of those glorious starts to the day that only seemed to manifest themselves during the early mornings in Dubai. Those of us who were especially lucky to live along the Creek were blessed with a grandstand view, as these mornings were truly magical.

At that time of the day the sun could be relied upon to be rising slowly over the desert, its rays gently gliding towards us and gradually playing a merry dance over the waters of the Creek, bathing the entire scene in a glorious rosy glow, engulfing one in its aura.

This sight was always accompanied by the cacophony of the various mullahs calling the faithful to prayer, their chanting eerily echoing over the rooftops adding a special dimension to early mornings in Dubai.

This was always a very special moment, in a very special place, which required one to stand back and gasp at the sheer wonder of it all and maybe make a note to rise early every morning to savour these splendid delights.

It brings to mind the song that Frank Sinatra sang so well, 'Chicago, Chicago, you're my kind of town'. I can honestly say that if the name were to be changed then guess what you would have — 'Dubai, Dubai, yes, you're my kind of town, I salute you'. Rest assured, I would be saying hello again tomorrow – same time, same place – Marsalamah.

What an enchanting start to my day and by my reckoning it should only get better. I was now all polished up and ready to motor to the airport. As I got closer I could feel strange vibes and everywhere was eerily silent. My goodness, something was up but what could be causing this tension in the air? As many of you know, in those far off days, Dubai International Airport wasn't exactly a flurry of activity, especially in the mornings but, oh my goodness, something strange was happening this particular morning. What was going on?

I parked as usual. Which bay should I use? There were so many to choose from, I virtually had the whole car park to myself. I sauntered up the steps, over the concourse and into the office. 'Who's for coffee?' was my usual greeting to the boys as I poked my head around the door.

This morning though, much to my utter astonishment, the office was chock-a-block. Oh my goodness, what was going on? My first thought was surely there wouldn't be enough coffee, milk or cups to go around. Who were these people and where, oh where, had they come from? I was swiftly marshalled into action and early that morning my first task wasn't to make copious cups of coffee as normal! Why was that, you may ask. All was then revealed!

It transpired that there had been rather a large skirmish between the Indians and the Pakistanis, somewhere over in the subcontinent, which necessitated all the BOAC flights flying to or from that zone to be diverted through Dubai whilst the situation could be assessed.

Naturally, it was necessary to know whether fighting was occurring in or around the airports used by BOAC. If so, a strategy would have to be worked out to enable the flights to be resumed as soon as possible, obviously avoiding the danger zones.

Naturally, this type of information gathering took time and, consequently, everyone our end had to be prepared to rally round. It was obvious that a situation like this would not or, indeed, could not be remedied overnight. I was first to be put into bat. Oh, what a mistake that was!

I was briefed about the situation and told that the arrivals lounge was stuffed full of people who didn't know what was going on, where they were in the world, and why on earth they were there in the first place. I was then packed off to pour oil over troubled waters.

One has to be reminded that in those far off days few people had heard of Dubai; consequently, these stranded passengers must have felt somewhat apprehensive, especially as when peering out of the vast windows of the arrivals lounge all they were able to see was desert. It wasn't too reassuring!

What could I do? I surely didn't know; in local parlance, the natives were getting fractious and my job was to calm them down! They were in for a treat! Instead of pouring oil on troubled waters, I think I possibly had the opposite effect and sent their collective blood pressures soaring!

In retrospect it was so funny. I was told to go and placate these poor passengers and do my bit for Queen and Country or was it Sheiks and sand dunes! So off I sallied in my usual fashion to be gobsmacked by what I found. Normally, the arrivals lounge would be frightfully busy with about twelve passengers waiting but that morning there seemed to be millions — I didn't know whether to laugh, cry or run for it.

How did I play this? It was definitely a new ball game for me. I was quickly spotted, which wasn't too difficult in my distinctive gear, and was pounced upon. 'Where are we? What are you organizing for us? When can we expect to arrive at our final destination?' On and on they burbled.

Quite naturally, I didn't know the answers to any one of their questions and when one man asked me what the current time was in London I looked blankly and said, 'Well, it's 8.30am here and we are four hours ahead!' And ran! Not very professional, I must admit!

As the day progressed, these passengers became more and more irate, particularly as I don't think any of them liked Arabic coffee too much or Fanta Orange, the only beverages being meted out at the little cafeteria on the concourse.

As for the lady who was normally in charge of the very basic catering facilities, she couldn't make it out at all, particularly when they were all shouting at her in English, 'I want Nescafé' or 'English tea' and 'oh yes, milk please and sugar, naturally'. As milk was normally of the evaporated kind from whence she came, a pantomime of gigantic proportions was erupting before my very eyes and I had no idea what to do about it!

Eventually, the airport caterers, who were situated in the bowels of the building, were press-ganged into action but, par for the course, they really were no better. As very few airlines uploaded meals from Dubai they didn't know how to jump to it pronto! I can't remember what they produced but it must have kept the wolf from the door because, to my knowledge, nobody collapsed in a heap!

I kept dashing back to the office and falling about with fits of the giggles, thinking it was all so terribly funny, only to be told to leap back into action. It was like being sent into the lion's den; quite terrifying.

Eventually, I managed to work out what the local time was in London. Understandably, they also wanted to know what the flying time was to London and if, as they hoped, they would depart in the next few hours what their ETA would be. Well, that really was a tricky one as actually I had no idea and nor had any of the operations staff as to when lift-off could be anticipated. I had never told so many white lies in my life, I am ashamed to say.

The boys in the office were not much better; they would dash out with their caps under their arms looking oh so smart and efficient, although they scuttled back as fast as their little legs would carry them because they too didn't know how to cope with the situation either. Thank goodness, I was not alone!

It took about three days for things to right themselves. It was quite amazing that a little dust-up between two neighbouring countries many, many miles from where we were could cause such havoc!

Unfortunately, when airline schedules are disrupted it takes quite a while to re-jig operations as there are so many ponderables to be taken into consideration — the actual position of the planes, crew availability, the uploading of fuel and, most importantly for the passengers, the victualing of the plane. Consequently, a disruption like this usually morphed into a gigantic logistical nightmare but was obviously not without amusing moments.

I very much doubt whether those stranded passengers, of whom they were many hundreds, thought it was funny at all once they had discovered that they were marooned for a time in the darkest desert.

It was, to them, possibly a Lawrence of Arabia moment, and we all know what happened to him! Maybe they thought that they would never see civilization again or even be eaten alive by something really, really nasty or, more terrifying, be stranded in the desert forever. My they would have got a lovely suntan though; I bet they hadn't thought of that!

Glorious desert photo
Image courtesy of "Marina Bruce, the desert diva"
Copyright holder

Another Chaotic Month!

We were now looking forward to another visit from my parents and I really hoped that this time I would have caught up with them in the expat stakes. It was possibly a vain hope, maybe a pipe dream but one could try one's damnedest, don't you think?

On reflection, my 18 months or so in the Persian Gulf were not really much for their nine years in Abadan in the 1930s; you definitely had to be made of stern stuff to survive that and come up smiling! My goodness, they most definitely were!

Naturally, there was excitement all round. Invitations were being extended and received and their diary was filling up rather rapidly; yes, they were a very popular couple.

We, on their behalf, even received an invitation to visit Mohammed Almulla's farm, as he so grandly called it. No, it wasn't quite on the other side of the moon but I feared it might be just as difficult to get to, as it was somewhere deep in the desert.

Mohammed Almulla was one of a handful of venerable locals who, in the early days, had made their living pearl diving and had now gravitated to running import and export businesses. He had acquired a small fleet of dhows, which were used to ply backwards and forwards to the subcontinent, quite often with substantial amounts of their cargo being gold bullion, a lucrative business indeed.

In those far off days, a British citizen was not allowed to hold gold bullion (I know not why); consequently, everything about Mohammed and his 'business' set-up seemed very daring to us!

It was as if even knowing him and being aware of some of these possibly clandestine operations we too were living dangerously! The Creek could, no doubt, have told many stories whilst it ebbed and flowed towards the Gulf.

Today, we were embarking on our very own adventure and it was about to begin. We set off on a hot Friday morning to weave our way into the desert and, if I'm honest, not having a clue on God's earth how we were ever going to find this homestead!

We, no doubt, would have had a far easier journey if we had gone by camel because surely they would have been happy to follow their noses and gallop along merrily. Alas, we had to make do with a very modern camel, our Toyota saloon – there were no four wheel drives in those days – which had to be encouraged and cajoled to make it over some of the rougher terrain. Happily it did with great stoicism, I am pleased to report!

After what seemed like an eternity of bumping, swerving, limping and spluttering, we spied a speck way in the distance and, oh please God, let it be journey's end, we couldn't stand this torture much longer.

Getting closer, we were not disappointed; yes, indeed it was an oasis and yes, hallelujah, we had actually found this pinprick in the middle of nowhere, more by luck than flaming judgement, wouldn't you agree? Big sighs of relief all round, thank you Allah!

There standing at the entrance to his hideaway was Mohammed, his face wreathed in smiles, no doubt heaving a great sigh of relief that he didn't have to send out a search party and the feeling was reciprocated! Beside him was a raggedy little Bedouin boy, who was about six years old.

We were told by Mohammed that this little chap was one of his sons of the desert. It was quite extraordinary because the majority of the Gulf Arabs were Bedouins and although they lived in the city and had, in the main, swapped their camels for Land Rovers they remained Bedouins at heart and the call of the desert remained very strong!

Mohammed's desert retreat was really an upmarket mud hut, which was surrounded by date palms, and plonked in the middle of this oasis was a rather large swimming pool. Yes, a little incongruous but, nevertheless, after our trek it was definitely a sight for sore eyes. Please, when can we jump in?

We were made very welcome although conversation was rather limited to say the least; there was no chewing the cud here, just chewing on the mutton grab feast that was produced. Our collective eyes nearly popped out of our heads when, from around the corner, two coolies appeared carrying an enormous tray on which languished a cooked goat surrounded by mountains of rice. Poor thing, it had, possibly, been happily galloping around a few hours earlier unaware of its impending fate. Such is life!

What a spectacle! When you are up front and personal with such an apparition, momentarily it takes your breath away and you are surely lost for words. Nothing could prepare one for the next part of this elaborate procedure either — they say there is a first time for everything!

No carving knife was needed as we witnessed, with utter astonishment, our host gauge out an eyeball ready to hand it to an honoured guest. One held one's breath not knowing whether to laugh, cry or make a dash for it, possibly headlong into the pool. There was no time either to detect the colour of the said delicacy — was it blue, green or brown? Actually, at that moment in time, I think that was the least of one's problems!

That was exactly what happened to us, with my mother being the honoured memsahib on this occasion; what a lucky lady she was! We stared in astonishment as she nonchalantly popped it into her mouth and swallowed it whole; how she managed it we will never know!

Would you believe she didn't immediately turn into Billy Goat Gruff either, an amazing achievement for the old girl. She should definitely have been in line for the highest award possible, a gold medal no less, but knowing Mama I think she would have preferred a giant bottle of Gordon's and, my goodness, she deserved every last drop!

After that little episode, knowing Mother had done her forfeit, as it were, the three of us were sitting terrified as to what we might be asked to do or eat. Thank goodness, we were spared and only had to eat freshly picked dates. We too rolled our eyes heavenwards realizing our prayers had actually been answered! Were we lucky, or were we lucky!

It was time to head off, not to the hills but from whence we came along those dusty tracks, which we hoped would – without too many diversions – lead us towards the head of the Creek and to downtown Dubai, our stamping ground!

This was not before Mother's new best friend had proffered yet another invitation. What a surprise; yes, you have guessed correctly, a nice friendly mutton grab but this time on board his special dhow, which would go for a gentle sail down to the mouth of the Creek before heading out into the Gulf.

Now, we were absolutely sure this would be a no-no as far as Mother was concerned because she suffered from terrible sea sickness. Well, what do you know, we were flabbergasted when we heard her saying, 'That would be lovely, can't wait'. Silly woman!

It was all arranged for the following Friday. How to waste one's only day off, hey ho, she who must be obeyed at all costs! Friday arrived and we set sail, the three of us in total trepidation as to how the next few hours would play out — we were not disappointed or surprised.

The dhow had hardly cast off before Naomi started to change colour, turning a lovely shade of green. We turned a blind eye. Here we go, we thought, knowing it would only get worse, especially as there was a live goat on board. It didn't take much of a wit to register that he wasn't long for this world because, yes, you have guessed, he was our lunch and destined for the pot! Oh dear, oh dear.

On one hand the deck boys were watching the pot and on the other peering at Naomi as she was gradually turning the colour of pea green. I must say the aromas wafting from the pot were enough to turn the strongest of wallahs pea green too!

As there was nowhere to go except overboard and swim for it, this little outing had to be endured. This we managed to do but it most definitely put us off going on another dhow trip for a very long time.

After what seemed like an eternity, we arrived back on dry land, more or less in one piece. We then gave Naomi a very stern lecture, saying that in future she had to consult all of us before she had any more crackpot ideas! I wasn't sure if she was listening, though!

We knew she liked receiving invitations – who doesn't – but this one had definitely been more like an endurance test and, yes, we were left to pick up the pieces. Please God, that was not to be repeated in a hurry!

We all know what curiosity does; yes, kills the cat but on this occasion it also turned the cat pea green.

An Audience!

Having got her off the dhow, over the road, up the steps and into the lift we were exhausted. No, it was not the cat's mother that we were attempting to bundle along but my dear Mama, who had excelled herself, letting the side down left, right and centre. After the stern lecture she received from the three of us, she retreated to her room repenting, we hoped!

Actually, she was so very disorientated after her sail up and down the Creek and her pallor definitely left a lot to be desired; would you believe, it was a deathly shade of green! Sadly, I didn't think she would remember or repent; we were resigned! But surely we could live in hope!

So, Mike and I continued as normal, getting up early, trotting off to work and being reunited over lunch, which was usually taken around 2.30pm.

Whilst my parents were with us we normally arrived back in a state of total trepidation wondering what Mother might have been up to during the morning — would she, I wondered, have hatched another plot and, if so, what would it be this time?

She had already made her mark by tagging along with the wives who had elected to help out at the Barasti refugee camps, which were situated far into the desert. These camps were the temporary home to many very sad illegal immigrants and were run under the auspices of the Save the Children Fund.

I have no doubt that these visits, together with the distribution of food parcels, would have lifted the spirits of these poor abandoned people. Thank goodness she was out of harm's way doing that and, for those few hours, we were able to breathe a sigh of relief and be thankful for small mercies!

On other occasions she would gaily announce that she had been asked to make up a fourth at bridge and sometimes these sessions started at 8am in the morning. Oh, what a to-do it all was trying to keep up with her!

My dear father used to sit quietly in the corner, pondering. Let's face it, having been married to Naomi for so many years he was surely used to being confronted by the unexpected on a regular basis. Now let me tell you about her next brainwave. Are you sitting comfortably, because you surely need to be!

As I previously mentioned, my parents were BP pensioners and BP was a prominent oil company in the Gulf with a good representation in Dubai. Without exception, the red carpet was rolled out for Naomi and Gordon, they were honoured guests wherever they went and, naturally, they were made especially welcome by the BP wallahs in Dubai.

Then it happened, calm before yet another proverbial storm! At one fateful party, Ma met a couple of locals, who obviously had connections with BP. We will never know just how the subject arose or, in fact, who broached it first, mind you I have a shrewd idea!

Never one to miss an opportunity, Mother suggested to these two that before her holiday was over she would really like to have an audience with Sheikh Rashid, the then ruler of Dubai and did they think such an idea would be possible? If so, how could it be arranged? Obviously, we didn't know what was going on otherwise she would have been bound and gagged!

Needless to say, she was full of this idea as Mike and I both quaked in our boots. She wouldn't stop talking about it and kept desperately trying to get in touch with her two latest chums. Unfortunately, one of them, Mohammed Al Moosa, owned a shop beneath our building – too close for comfort – and the other, Zacheriah Doley, lived in a pagoda which he had built some way out in the desert and was a little difficult to miss; consequently, they were sitting ducks.

It was all becoming very tricky indeed, with me thinking Mike would get the sack or maybe he would find a shotgun and shoot Mother as, at this stage, it might possibly be the only sure way of deterring her. We knew it was a vain hope that she would have second thoughts and let the matter drop, as this definitely wasn't her style. What were we going to do?

The rows that ensued were nobody's business; she wouldn't be deterred as she was hell-bent on this, her latest mission, and this was to have an audience with Sheikh Rashid, right reason or none. I was sick with worry, Mike was as mad as hell and I seem to remember that my poor father had taken to lunging for soothing whiskies. No I'm not joking, our nerves were in tatters!

You had to hand it to Naomi, she was like a dog worrying a bone and, with an immense amount of cajoling, she managed to get her 'mission impossible' up and running. To this day, I don't know how she did it, as she was definitely flying solo on this occasion!

Somehow, she had managed to rally Zacheriah Doley and Mohammed Al Moosa and announced that they would be calling for her in a couple of days' time to escort her to the Majlis, where the ruler usually received his visitors.

It didn't even cross her mind that Sheikh Rashid might not be too happy inviting her into his inner sanctum such was her determination and, I might add, enthusiasm. We departed for our respective offices, I remember, being almost too terrified to return home that lunchtime in case she had been shot by the firing squad or Mike had got the sack or even carted off to jail.

Well, what do you know! She returned to the fold, bursting with pride; yes, being Naomi she had more than accomplished her mission. She had been received by Sheikh Rashid and he had even allowed one of her chums to take a photo, which he subsequently signed for her.

Phew! Yes, we had to hand it to her, naturally she was the talk of the town and nothing was going to stop her now. Surely she couldn't have any more Desperate Dan ideas up her sleeve or could she?

I do have to mention, though, that for some unknown reason she had taken to wearing wigs. I think she thought donning a wig was very much easier than whizzing to the hairdresser every five minutes and this was another little eccentricity of hers. Of course, this day was no exception; thank God it didn't blow away with the excitement of everything or take-off with all the hot air that was being generated.

Once she had come down to earth and we both realized that neither of us had got the sack or were in jail, she recounted just how the morning had progressed. Mohammed Al Moosa and Zacheriah Doley had driven her to the Majlis, which was situated beside the Creek in Bur Dubai, the other side of the Creek from us.

Actually, a Majlis is a meeting room where, in this case, the locals who for some reason or another would like an audience with the Sheikh would sit and wait in the hope that they would be called forth. Obviously, a few strings had been pulled that morning but this is where Naomi found herself sitting alongside Bedouins and local businessmen waiting her turn whilst being surrounded by armed guards who I believe she kept telling to stand to attention. Thank goodness we were far, far away at the time to know what was going on.

Eventually, her dream came true and she was ushered into the inner sanctum to be introduced to Sheikh Rashid. I believe she sat with the Sheikh for a while and, through the help of an interpreter, she mentioned having lived in Abadan in the Thirties and attending the then Shah's wedding.

Yes, they enjoyed a common bond, the love of the desert, which undoubtedly shone through and must have bathed their meeting in a warm glow as it surely was a wondrous occasion for Naomi and indeed supremely unique for Sheikh Rashid.

As far as any of us are aware, Naomi was the first lady ever to be received by Sheikh Rashid in his Majlis and I have serious doubts if many more have ever followed in her footsteps.

Naturally, Naomi was simply delighted and we were left dumbfounded. Oh, Mother, you did it again!

Lying in a Darkened Room!

How did one recover from a whirlwind of majestic proportions, I was asking myself. I supposed the obvious answer would be to go and lie in a darkened room until the feeling had passed and that I was quite certain I was back on an even keel.

Mind you, the way I felt I was positive that I would be lying in the darkened room for a very, very long time. Not only was my head thumping but I think my whole body was shaking as a consequence of all the shenanigans.

Unfortunately, I really had no time to lie in a darkened room; the show had to go on. What show, I can hear you asking. Well, I will tell you. Naomi had just taken her last bow and the curtain had come down on her final act; more to the point, her grand finale!

I would never have been able to second guess that just getting her to the airport and into the departure lounge would have been so traumatic. Yes, some would say it was definitely her last hoorah, and what a hoorah it proved to be!

I had been left to gather my scattered wits, terrified that she was already pencilling in her next debut onto the Dubai stage. 'Please God; don't let it be too soon, I don't think I can cope. Actually I know I can't!' I was weak at the knees thinking that it may even be a possibility.

You might recall my mother didn't seem to be too much like other mamas, well not the ones I had had the pleasure of meeting. She didn't appear to give a damn about anything (I mean this in the nicest possible way). If she got an idea into her head she pursued it with the tenacity of a terrier. Off she went, right reason or none.

Between you and me, I was fully expecting Mike to come home that afternoon to say that he was well and truly in the doghouse with Shell and I thought that, perhaps, BOAC would want to know what all the commotion was about at check-in that morning.

Actually, it was my ma trying to get an enormous five-foot by three-foot oil painting of the Creek, incidentally still in its frame, on board their flight to London as hand luggage, no less!

I ask you, it never crossed her mind that it might be too large to even get through the cabin door, let alone that she might have been charged excess baggage; how dire would that have been. Between you and me, I had a shrewd idea that somehow she would have tried to sidestep that issue too. No wonder I was in such a pickle!

To think she even bamboozled her way into the Majlis and actually had an audience with Sheikh Rashid. Secretly I was full of admiration but wished she hadn't had these bright ideas on my watch.

We will never know how she met Mohammed Al Moosa or, for that matter, Zacheriah Doley let alone how she managed to coerce them into being party to this deadly deed. It was obviously bribery of some sort or another or, by any chance, did she still have a twinkle in her eye that totally mesmerized the pair of them?

I do know she gave them both a special silver coin that had been minted in London to commemorate a particular royal occasion, as a thank you. I think Zacheriah had his made into a key ring! A memento indeed! I'm sure the last time I saw him he said that it was still in use, a daily reminder of an amazing moment with one amazing lady!

I wondered when it would be safe to get out from under; well, what I really meant was to show myself around town. I was a bit apprehensive really, wondering how many other people might come forth with a 'little gem' about her. I surely didn't want to know.

I had a vision of whoever her next victim might be saying, 'Here she comes — one, two, three, duck!' Actually, I wasn't too sure if I was up to hearing about any more of her antics; it was best to let sleeping dogs lie.

I had heard though that when she tagged along with the lady benefactors, who used to rise at the crack of dawn and drive way out into the desert to 'feed the children', that she had them all singing songs from the Sound of Music as they marched over the desert.

This surely must have been a sight and a sound to behold, especially as the sun would have just been rising over the horizon, bathing this merry little scene with its rosy glow. And so it went on! I wasn't too sure how the devil I managed to be so normal! Or was I?

As the saying goes, the show must go on. Time had stood still for the last month and there were things to do. Firstly, I had to regain my equilibrium then leap off to the sailing club; my poor Minisail would be feeling truly abandoned. I had just remembered that I had offered to take one of the new Army wives out for a spin; she would be thinking that I had stood her up, oh dear!

Invitations were still piling up on our proverbial mantelpiece — sometimes I felt as if I had to keep running just to stand still. With new military arrivals popping up here and there all wanting to become part of the Dubai social scene there was no shortage of smart military parties to be attended. As the saying goes, there is no show without Punch!

A little secret — the dinner parties we gave usually started off by being pretty formal but had a tendency to degenerate as the evening wore on. I wonder why? This was especially apparent when the time arrived for the ladies to take their leave whilst the men enjoyed that age old ritual of passing the port; naturally, always to the left!

Our lady guests were never backwards in coming forwards and were usually quite miffed at being shunted off, adopting the attitude that if you can't join them you might as well match them, thus demanding a large top-up to enjoy whilst powdering their noses!

More often than not the houseboys had pre-empted their requests thus ensuring the girls definitely did not lose out on valuable drinking time. One of these days maybe we girls would have our own ritual of passing the port whilst powdering our noses; now that was definitely a thought! These ladies were a formidable bunch and didn't need telling that there was normally more than one way of killing the cat!

I thought I was now beginning to recover and might raise my head above the parapet and have a little peek at the outside world. As I looked down on the dhows below, gently bobbing up and down with the ebb and flow of the tide, I could see their inhabitants busying themselves with their daily routines. Thank goodness, it all seemed so reassuringly normal.

I heaved a great sigh of relief, as I thought I might just be feeling brave enough to face the outside world. Then I had a strange thought — maybe they were the only folk in Dubai that my mama didn't try and chat up, or did she? I have news for you, I wasn't going to stick my neck out, and so we will never know!

Just recalling my mother's antics has made me want to go and lie in a darkened room, even after all these years!

Pottering About!

Invitations were flying through the proverbial letter box at a rate of knots. How we ever had time to go to work, I really don't know! Now then, if I should be asked to give just one piece of advice to any prospective new arrival, I would most definitely say pack your dancing shoes and hit the ground running.

On a cautionary note though, if you don't have leanings towards being a party animal then, possibly, the Dubai we found ourselves in will not be the place for you.

How was one to know though? It was not so long ago when we felt sure that the only thing happening in this place, with absolute certainty, was that the Creek was continually ebbing and flowing and that the dhows were coming and going.

There seemed to be only one course of action open to us which was to climb aboard, adjust our water wings and go with the flow. Ours was a different sort of flow, though, and the flotsam and jetsam that were being washed up in our wake was the debris we had created after yet another night on the town!

To this day, I am totally astonished that a small kingdom such as Dubai could have been so frenetic, although initially it was not apparent and obviously a closely guarded secret. One had to be taken by the hand and led gently along for all to be revealed.

The starting point for all of us was obviously the airport, and I'm sure I would be correct in saying that there would have been many a reluctant debutant being led towards the parking area quaking in their boots, wondering just what lay before them and if they would be able to cope.

There were no surprises on the road leading away from the airport towards the town. Actually, the road was quite ordinary, a modest two-lane highway, bordered by oleanders which had been planted, I think, to cunningly mask the encroaching desert. This straight stretch of road was broken up by a couple of roundabouts with one road leading off to Sharjah on the right and if you were happy to turn left you would pass over the Al Maktoum Bridge and be on your way to Jumeirah, that exulted suburb by the sea.

Come to think of it, I'm not too sure why it wasn't referred to as Jumeirah-on-Sea, rather like some of the seaside towns in the UK, such as Littlehampton-on-Sea. That would have given the place a little panache surely more fitting to the status it aspired to as the Riviera of Dubai, which even in those days was such a sought after address!

Jumeirah was really a cluster of villas huddling between two quasi-main roads which ran horizontal to the sea; one was the beach road, where Spinneys the Supermarket was located, and the other we called the Iranian Hospital Road. Obviously, there were numerous interconnecting roads but I can tell you without a shadow of a doubt there was an awful lot of sand around and about!

It's hard to imagine, I know, but parking up outside Spinneys could have been akin to driving up to a supermarket in the Wild West. One drove off the tarmac road onto sand, screeched to a halt in front of the main entrance and sauntered in — there was no by your leave or how's your father there!

There was no designated parking in those days, just sand, sand and more glorious sand. There was also another supermarket opposite, called Gulf Trading, I think. There you have it, there was no fancy shopping; it was take it or leave it! Normally, one had to take it because there was truly no alternative.

A little further down from Spinneys was a zoo. To this day I have no idea why Jumeirah was lucky enough to have a zoo in its midst. On reflection, that was Dubai for you, it was full of surprises! Whoever the mystery benefactor was, he or she certainly gave a lot of pleasure to many, many people.

Reflecting on events, maybe the zoo was the first glimmer that not too far buried beneath all that sand lay some enterprising minds and, as we now know, ideas soon began to flourish and blossom rather rapidly, with quite spectacular results.

In the early 1970s, the beach road in Jumeirah ended just past Spinneys with the tarmac finishing abruptly, giving way to desert, and that was that. The same applied to the Iranian Hospital Road, as it was known to us, which was the only other main tarmac road leading towards Abu Dhabi.

No surprises there — it fell far short of its destination as it too was only about two kilometres long and then morphed into desert. Camels still had the best deal in that neck of the woods, surely making short work of getting to Abu Dhabi.

The Iranian Hospital was a complete enigma to most of us, possibly except for the locals and those of Iranian origin, of which there were many living in Dubai. Its side entrance was on the road to Satwa, a charming little 'village' in English parlance, which was nestled between two main roads.

Even in those days it was a well-established trading post, inhabited mostly by Indians and Pakistanis, all shopkeepers, selling anything and everything; it was a veritable Aladdin's cave.

These little 'holes in the wall' called dukas – shops to you and me – were a delight and one never ceased to be amazed at the variety of goods on offer, such as gigantic cooking pots that were big enough for a goat to happily rest in before meeting its fate. There were also perfumes of dubious origins, with one whiff guaranteed to knock you for six straight out of the door and maybe headlong into a passing camel! Oh my, it was surely a shopping experience with a difference.

One could never go far on a little sortie into Satwa without relishing the aromas wafting along the street from the various eating establishments, of which there were many. The most famous of them all was Ravi's, a wonderful curry house loved by locals and expats alike, and I am delighted to report that to this day it is still going strong. Bravo!

If you were not a curry lover then it had to be one of the many little places offering Arabic delights, such as hummus, fatoush, baba ganoush and, of course, kebabs all washed down with a glass of fresh orange — oh the magic.

I would say, though, it was not so magical for the poor cooks who worked in appalling conditions, which were as hot as hell. How they ever produced such tasty treats with a smile on their faces, I will never know! But they did, and I have no doubt still do, to the delight of all their customers both past and present, many of whom are now scattered all over the globe.

Before we leave this little corner I must mention the other people that made up this hard-working community, people that no fashion conscious memsahib could have coped without, and they were the tailors. They naturally walked hand in hand with the numerous material shops selling amazing silks, satins, sari material, and bolts of fine black and white cotton from which dishdashas and abayas were fashioned; in fact, there was something for everyone, even little old me!

To get this particular show on the road, one had to have a tailor, naturally guarding his name closely, thus keeping the memsahibs guessing and hopefully giving the sometimes very misleading impression that you had stumbled across Satwa's answer to Christian Dior or that your latest little number just might have been purchased in Paris!

This prompted your 'chums' to exclaim, 'My dear, it couldn't possibly have been fashioned in that sandy enclave called Satwa, or could it? How on earth can we find out?' Yes, on occasions women can be devious little devils!

First things first, having netted your tailor it was time to set up a meeting to discuss requirements, take measurements, haggle on prices and determine the finishing date.

Armed with every conceivable detail it was time for the off, which would entail visiting almost every material shop in the whole of Satwa, scurrying around here, there and everywhere to try and bag the latest offerings. This surely wasn't an exercise in keeping up with the Joneses — it was about keeping one step ahead, a very serious task indeed!

Naturally, we took all this for granted never giving a thought as to how amazing it was to be able to walk away from this little sandy street clutching your latest must-have. This could easily have been a copy of a little Dior number that you had seen in a magazine or maybe a copy of a very expensive outfit which you had acquired in London whilst on leave.

Our whims and wishes were normally accommodated with great patience, as I'm sure on occasions we acted like spoilt little brats, never realizing just how fortunate we were to have this expertise on our doorstep.

On reflection, these chaps were surely amazing; where they learnt their trade had to be a mystery. The conditions under which they worked left a lot to be desired too, with many of them stitching away whilst sitting cross-legged on the floor, day in and day out.

The collective tailoring talent that had found its way to this little corner of Dubai was surely extraordinary, with most of these chaps emanating from little villages in India or Pakistan. Yes, they too were far from home and, indeed, surely out of their comfort zone.

They had to be applauded for their desire to slowly climb the greasy pole of life, which for them had possibly started there, in downtown Satwa, such a long, long way from that place they called home.

A Favour Please, Jan!

We coasted through the first couple of months of 1972 reflecting on all the happenings that had recently taken place. Actually, if I am honest, we needed time to lick our wounds, take stock and regroup. I know we had nothing to do with the services but we felt as if we had been on a very tricky outward bound course for which, on occasions, we were sadly ill-equipped. No wonder we were feeling a little worse for wear; do I dare tell you that we had recently received and attended 34 party invitations in one month. Now that's what I call having stamina; after all, it would have been rude not to!

We were gradually surfacing and cracking on with life. Me with my sailing and dotting off to the airport each morning and Mike with his golf together with looking after his Bitumen Supply Company, which also entailed travelling around the Gulf.

My mornings where never short of surprises and they were always made especially memorable when the 'boys' from Masirah pitched up. To put you in the picture, Masirah is an island in the Indian Ocean, just off the coast of Oman, and was used as a staging post for the RAF; consequently, it required troops on the ground in the form of RAF personnel.

As Masirah was plonk in the middle of the deep blue yonder, it was necessary to carry out a weekly 'shopping run' up to Dubai to purchase anything and everything, which also enabled the 'boys' to let off a little steam. Initially, I really didn't take too much notice when these chaps used to boisterously cascade through our office door, their handlebar moustaches twitching in anticipation of the delights they might just be about to sample downtown.

As these visits were on a regular basis I soon became acquainted with the antics of this happy crew; they always seemed to be game for a laugh and their enthusiasm was infectious. They were certainly never backwards in coming forwards. It didn't take them long to register that they could possibly have a very good stooge in the form of little old me, if they played their cards right, maybe ready to run an errand or two for them in their absence. I wasn't in a position to refuse their bizarre requests, or at least I didn't think I was; I was too polite really but I should have known better!

Actually, it was a wonder I didn't get the sack or at least be sent to the Empty Quarter because they really got me in such a fix this last particular time. It just shows how bored they must have been whiling away their days on Masirah with little to do except sunbathe and, I think, play the odd game of cricket against the locals using oil drums as wickets!

This particular day I should have known something was up as the door was slowly opened and being wheeled in behind the first chap was a bloody great motorbike; in retrospect it was a wonder he wasn't riding it and tooting the horn at the same time, such was their irreverence. A breath of fresh air if one was needed!

I looked up wondering what was happening. All was then revealed — one of the chaps had recently purchased the said bike in the Souk and shipped it back to Masirah and it now wouldn't go, possibly gunged up with sand, but who was I to state the possibly blindingly obvious. They were on a mission and were taking it back from whence it came to see what could be done to rectify the situation. Off they went having arrived through one door and now sallying forth out of the other, I might add straight through the boss's office – motorbike and all – well that was par for the course!

I didn't think any more about this little meeting but later that day there was a rat-tat-tat on our front door and, much to my surprise, there stood all five of said RAF personnel looking very sheepish indeed. What now? Yes, I know, they wanted a beer and Apartment 603 was their best bet. They shuffled in, slightly nervously. What was going on? As they were so quiet and even their moustaches were motionless they were most definitely up to no good.

I was right, oh my goodness, I suppose I should have been flattered by being treated as one of the 'boys' but sometimes it became a little too much. I was about to find out this was definitely going to one of those occasions when I would have preferred to be just one of the girls.

Once they had found their voices, their opening gambit was would I, could I, possibly do them a big favour and get them out of a real jam; yes, I was the proverbial sitting duck! Then all was revealed. Did I recall that they had had a motorbike with them this morning? Well, something was very wrong with it and it had to be left at the motorbike hospital to be resuscitated. Yes? 'Well, it won't be ready for five days and then it will have to be collected,' was the reply.

'So what?' I said.

'Actually, this is where, please dear Jan, you come in.'

'But I don't know how to ride a motorbike.'

'No you don't have to, we told the chap in the shop to deliver it into your care at the BOAC office in the airport.'

I must have been hearing things. I didn't know whether to laugh or cry — was it cheek or was it an enormous compliment. Whatever it was, I seemed to be part of this escapade whether I liked it or not!

They explained that the shop wasn't in a position to store the bike after it had been repaired and, as I knew, they wouldn't be back in town for seven days and consequently a resting place was required for two days. They couldn't think of anywhere else for the wretched bike to be tethered other than BOAC's front office which, unfortunately, just happened to be the boss's office too.

I went as white as a sheet and nearly fainted to boot. I knew I was a brick but this suggestion was quite outrageous and also totally out of the question; after all, I had to conduct myself with a modicum of decorum, my reputation was at stake and also my job. What to do?

It was quite obvious that before they had even ratted on the door I was a goner. The plan went like this, 'Today is Wednesday, the bike will be ready next Sunday but we won't be around until Tuesday. We have told the chap to go to the airport on Sunday morning around about 11am, after the VC10 has departed for London, knock on the door and ask for you. Yes, once you have been located, they will wheel the bike in and hand you the necessary papers together with the ignition key for safekeeping'. I suppose I must be thankful for small mercies, thank God they didn't mention riding it in at full throttle. 'Then hopefully, you don't mind, do you, keeping it under wraps for a couple of days? Be a sport, please?'

It seemed I had no option. How could I be a party pooper? But I was just a little apprehensive to say the least, as I think any normal person just might be!

I was on tenterhooks. Sunday duly arrived – actually I hoped it wouldn't – and, yes, there was a knock on the door, which was answered by one of the young duty airport managers. Naturally they were in on this dirty deed as they were always game for a laugh!

I will never know who fell about laughing first but there sitting in front of my boss's desk was the biggest bloody motorbike you could ever have imagined and I was in charge of it for two days! The boys thought it was totally hysterical but what about Ken, our boss; what did we do? Boys being boys, they shrugged and wandered back to their flight plans, leaving me in a total panic.

All I could do was vainly hope that Ken might be taken ill for the next two days. Obviously that was to be a pipe dream as it wasn't too long before he flung open his office door, looking at us all in blank astonishment. He then asked, so very politely, as to how this obvious piece of lost property had found its way into his office and did I/we have any ideas? We all looked around sheepishly and then, as one, collapsed in merriment. Dear Ken had clocked us many moons ago and had long since given up on us all and it wasn't even April Fools' Day!

I was first in the firing line, spluttering and whimpering that I was so sorry but what could I do, my hands were tied, naturally in the name of Queen and Country. I had to help the RAF, maybe the bike was being used on secret missions around Masirah. It wasn't very convincing but what else was there to say. The boys tried their best, only making matters worse. In the meantime, to add to the confusion, a plane was heading in from Bombay and a flight plan had to be detailed pronto for the onward leg to London. Please God, they don't re-route the plane via Outer Mongolia in the confusion, I thought.

There was silence; obviously the only thing I could do was to say sorry but also said I was quite sure he wouldn't mind sharing his office with a motorbike for two days, as between us we would surely be mentioned in dispatches. I was also certain that a letter of thanks would already be winging its way from the Air Vice-Marshal concerned, offering thanks. A vain hope!

Two days can be a very long time when you are in the doghouse, but Tuesday eventually arrived with the boys once again bouncing through the office door, moustaches swivelling as usual. They were very solicitous, naturally, knowing they were in for a good hiding but still had mischief in their eyes. 'Only a few hours, dear Jan, then we will get that bloody machine out of your hair.' Thank God it was Ken's day off!

With that they dashed downtown with their usual urgency but, thank goodness, as promised they were back rather smartly, asking for the key to the front office to enable them to wheel the bike through and off towards their transport.

Wonderful, amazing — we were all still alive and I still had my job, but it didn't quite end there. One of the chaps said, 'Hi Jan, how about riding pillion down the whirligig, over the apron and up to our plane; it will be a bit of fun'.

Golly gosh, I'm nothing if not totally daft but game for a laugh all the same. Off I went and, yes, I did ride pillion down the whirligig, over the tarmac right up to their waiting plane and, no, I didn't get the sack and wasn't even threatened with being sent to the Empty Quarter — now that really was a very close shave!

A *Fishy Business!*

The day began, as usual, with great expectations, but I would wager along with a hangover. It was Friday morning after all and without a doubt we would have been tripping the light fantastic somewhere around this desert kingdom, along with many a happy playmate.

Amazingly, last night we actually did something very different, which we all thought extremely novel; after all, one had to ring the changes somehow! A few weeks back a plot was hatched, which went like this:

'Why don't we enquire about hiring an abra for an evening, or maybe two, depending on the number of people who are up for this stunt?' What a good idea! Leisurely floating up and down the Creek whilst enjoying a picnic would surely be a splendid way of spending a happy evening, and one with a difference to boot, how original!

Actually, the planning went like clockwork as we had not taken into account that the abra skippers were only too eager to earn a little extra dosh. Grand picnics were planned and assembled but, alas, not a wicker basket was in sight. In retrospect, I'm not too sure what was packed because, as you will know by now, it was not exactly easy to be inventive with the produce that we had at our disposal in those early days.

On occasions ringing in the new year would have been easier than ringing the changes to our menus. I will have a bet with you though, I'm sure the picnic would have included hard boiled eggs and chicken of some description, and I reckon that to date we have eaten chicken cooked and presented every which way, all washed down with copious amounts of booze, of course.

We assembled at the abra crossing on the Deira side where our two abras were moored and the skippers were waiting. Before you get any grand ideas, it wasn't like stepping onto a gondola from the bank of a Venice canal and, no, the chaps were most definitely not wearing special livery, far from it, nor were they geared up to serenading us with their very own rendition of 'O Sole Mio'. The nearest we got to being serenaded was by the mullahs calling the faithful to prayer together with the gentle lapping of the water as we drifted slowly upstream.

This was to be a romantic evening with us embarking on a lovely, improvised glide up the Creek, hoping for a full moon to guide us on our way, nothing less, but we had over looked one very important factor.

Abras are not designed for leisurely sails but quick sprints across the water from one side of the Creek to the other. My goodness it was uncomfortable and we had not thought to bring travelling rugs; mind you, I very much doubt if any of us would have possessed such a thing, let alone a blanket or two. Consequently, we were rattling around on the bottom of the boat feeling exceedingly uncomfortable and more than a little cold; in fact, if I recall correctly we were frozen to death.

Our skippers must have thought we were all stark raving mad; in fact, it didn't take too long for us to concur. Even the lights mischievously twinkling over the water didn't do much to take our minds off our bruised and decidedly uncomfortable bodies and, as for the picnic, well do you think the little morsels that were produced could ease our discomfort? Actually, you are quite right, they didn't! Once again, dear Mr Gray Mackenzie was at hand, coming to our rescue so, thank goodness, all was not lost!

We awoke on Friday morning feeling decidedly battered and bruised but, after licking our wounds, began contemplating our day. It was wondrous; we had a whole day stretching out before us, a treat indeed. We marshalled our scattered wits, admired the various bruises we had acquired whilst bumping up and down in the abra and then realized we had no time to lose if we were going to get to Al Hamriya in time for another jolly picnic, which once again would be washed down with some of the goodies that Mr Gray Mac would be laying on; he was such a kind and thoughtful person!

Al Hamriya was a favourite haunt for our Friday awaydays. It was a little fishing village up the coast, a little way out of Sharjah. It had little to offer except sun, sea and sand but in those days that was all we required together with a few chums and the aforementioned victuals to have fun. I was about to say that we usually managed to make the most of what was available, which was a good thing, because there was very little in the way of light entertainment in those far off days.

We sure made the most of our Fridays. They were lazy, hazy days, dipping in and out of the water at regular intervals, which was so necessary to cool off; yes, it was always decidedly hot and, on reflection, I'm not too sure how much sun lotion we ever used. Maybe it had not been invented then! Only joking, or am I?

I do recall some bright spark proffering a mixture of oil and lemon juice, announcing that it did wonders for the skin, whilst definitely encouraging a golden tan — we couldn't resist, lathering it on with gusto. We secretly hoped that overnight we would be transformed — into what? Well, I'm still not quite sure. Oh I know, real glamour girls, or maybe we thought we were just basting the proverbial goose, who knows, but it was fun!

There was one further little ritual that we had to participate in and that was keeping a keen eye out for the green flash. What on earth was that, I can hear you saying. Well, after enjoying our day wallowing around in the water, also inspecting and marvelling at the banks of discarded oyster shells which had collected over the years – these being a by-product of the once thriving pearling industry – and then possibly looking for shells which had been washed up to add to our collections, it was time to take a seat on the nearest sand dune to wait for the wondrous 'green flash', the grand finale of our day.

Now for the uninitiated, this phenomenon only occurs as the setting sun dips below the horizon, yes really, but I have to say one blink and it's gone and sadly you will have missed it yet again! Now honestly, how many times is that?

To this day I'm not sure whether the green flash actually exists — is it a myth, perhaps, a fantasy or a touch of the blarney? Whatever, this was a ritual enacted every Friday and heaven help anybody who disputed its very existence!

Our team leader for this grand spectacle was a truly wonderful lady who would have us believe that she saw it on every single occasion and also, I think, had seen it on every single continent. We were in awe and did our best but it was never quite good enough!

Hot and happy, we bade adieu to Al Hamriya for another week and headed down the Sharjah road back to Dubai. It was time to shake the sand out of our hair and regroup to ensure that we were bright-eyed and bushy-tailed for the start of what would more than likely be another busy week.

Every so often things didn't go according to plan and this particular Friday evening was to illustrate this point admirably. To this day I will never know where the dreaded packet of smoked haddock fillets came from; obviously, as far as I was concerned, they were definitely a 'must have' when I spied them lurking somewhere in the depths of Spinneys' or Hassani's freezers. I'm sure I would have said to Mike, 'We are in for an absolute treat tonight — smoked haddock with a poached egg on top!' Lovely, but we didn't bargain for what ensued.

Taking one mouthful and languidly drooling over the magnificent taste I suddenly spluttered and, to my great dismay, seemed to have a dreaded fish bone stuck in my throat! For what seemed like an eternity I coughed, spluttered and choked with disastrous consequences. Mike was running around like a headless chicken whilst I was thinking that, perhaps, I was about to become a legless chicken!

Medical facilities in those early days were sparse and neither of us could think of what to do or where to go; surely everything would be better in the morning. We survived the night, with difficulty, and then it was action stations. After many phone calls and exchanges of information it was deduced that there was only one ENT chap in the Gulf and he was in Bahrain, not exactly round the corner!

By this time, from what I can recall, the whole of the Gulf had been alerted as to my plight.

All stops were pulled out and I soon found myself fastening my seat belt, having been rapidly dispatched on a plane to Bahrain. On arrival I was met by kind colleagues from BP, who all seemed to be dashing around with worried expressions on their faces. Between you and me, I think they thought they were going to meet a corpse, so no red carpet! What a shame!

I felt such a fraud, but knew I had better play along with all this because by the time they had shoved me through the doctor's door, I do think the bone had become dislodged. I didn't dare say a word but the doctor chap agreed and said he couldn't detect any obstruction but to oil the wheels, as it were, suggested that all would be very much better if I partook of a soothing ice cold gin and tonic, which as we all know is usually the cure for most things! He was so right!

I never did dare admit that, perhaps, it had all been a figment of my imagination and that maybe the excitement of waiting for the green flash and missing it once again had completely addled my brain, sending me into a tiswas of monumental proportions; who knows! It was definitely an awayday with a difference!

Dining at the Ritz!

And a Nightingale Sang!

It was spring 1972 and we were hurtling towards our second leave; the time had flown by. Two years ago, I would have had my doubts that I would have still been around to utter these words, let alone with a smile on my face; how wrong I was. What I wanted to know is if we could spare the time to go on leave? What a daft question, I can hear you saying. Actually, I wasn't so sure!

In the two years we had been there, we had witnessed and also been part of some amazing changes which, quite naturally, had made our lives so very much more enjoyable. The major change was obviously the opening of the Country Club, where the longed-for golf course was being put through its paces on a daily basis by the avid golfers in our midst.

Up until that moment it had been tough going, as recreational facilities were extremely limited — there was the swimming pool at the Bustan Hotel and, of course, miles and miles of beautiful sandy beaches. Naturally, if swimming wasn't your preferred sport you were up a proverbial gum tree, although you could have enjoyed a Heineken or two whilst wallowing in the shallows along with the rest of us.

I was so very fortunate being able to make use of the little sailing club tucked down beside the Al Maktoum Bridge, without which I am utterly convinced I would have gone stark staring mad!

There was also a new attraction and that was the incarnation of the Abu Dhabi road, which provided thrills and spills galore. There was no bouncing over the desert these days, you just whizzed over the Al Maktoum Bridge, drove straight ahead for a mile or so and you would then connect with the new road; yes, that's it folks, 'Abu Dhabi here we come'. You could then put your foot down and hope for the best that, at the very least, a herd of camels wouldn't decide to dash across your path and also that you wouldn't encounter a very excited local who had abruptly abandoned his camel for a shiny limo.

Needless to say, he possibly wouldn't have had the first clue as to how to drive as no driving tests were required; don't be silly, the ignition was turned on and off they sped. Yes, it was the devil take the hindmost. You had to hope and pray that you wouldn't encounter one of these madcap drivers on your travels. Actually, I wasn't too sure which was the most terrifying, a four-legged camel or a two-legged local.

If you didn't relish a boring Friday cowering indoors trying to avoid the searing heat you could always join a Wadi Bashing party. I found myself on one such expedition and between you and me thought the whole experience to be quite excruciating. They say ignorance is bliss but for the life of me I couldn't imagine a worse way to spend a day; I know, I know, I'm a heathen!

For the uninitiated, a wadi is a dried-up riverbed, its main component being boulders which come in various shapes and sizes thus providing an extremely bumpy ride. I would advise anybody embarking on such an expedition not to have eaten beforehand! I rest my case!

It goes without saying that it would have been rude to turn down such a wonderful invitation, especially coming from our TOS chums, who knew the territory inside out. We were assured that we would be in safe hands and that we would have the time of our lives!

I had been told on numerous occasions how enchanting wadis were, that they were host to masses of flora and fauna, unlike the desert. I was intrigued, especially as there was a dearth of vegetation on our normal stamping grounds. In retrospect, I should have stuck to my tried and trusted desert tracks, then at least I could have bailed out when the going got tough and wouldn't have had to hang on for dear life thinking that, maybe, my end was nigh. Please God, or is it Allah, get me out of here! Pronto! I have important news for anyone who cares to listen; you can leave me behind next time, thank you so very much.

I thought that maybe I had moaned and groaned enough to ensure that I would be excluded from any more of these hair-raising excursions; I was so wrong. This time it was a camping trip somewhere on the seashore beyond Ras Al Khaimah; yes, once again my arm was twisted being told that it would be a wonderful experience, silly me! Obviously, we didn't possess any camping gear, not even a billycan; no problem, we were told, as it was another trusted Army exercise and everything would be adequately taken care of!

This time, we had to set sail at lunchtime on Thursday, rendezvousing somewhere in Sharjah, with the idea of arriving at our destination in the late afternoon, which turned out to be a little sandy beach complete with rock pools nestling under a mountain range. Well, well, so far so good; who on earth had discovered this lovely little spot? We'd better watch out — were we possibly being lulled into a false sense of security?

The camp was set up with very little help from me! I didn't know one end of a guy rope from another. There seemed to be an awful lot to organize but, as the afternoon sauntered into early evening, sundowners were eagerly being anticipated, and these were sipped and savoured whilst once again marvelling at yet another glorious sunset, for which the Gulf is justifiably renowned — green flash or not; it was just stunning!

Goodness knows what was on the menu but suffice to say we didn't starve. I was just about to say, 'So far so good', but as day turned into night it was the signal for the mosquitoes to make their presence felt; oh my goodness, how did one combat these little perishes? The answer was that one didn't. What were we to do? Not a lot because even dashing into the sea was a little problematic as there may have been lurking sharks. Discretion was definitely the better part of valour, as on this occasion the mosquitoes were possibly the lesser of the two evils!

It was now time to retire and another tricky situation presented itself as us girls were allocated the tent whilst the boys were going to be kipping around and about. It seemed fair enough but it was stiflingly hot in the tent so we abandoned it rather smartly. I don't really need to tell you but a most uncomfortable night was endured by one and all. I couldn't quite get my head around all this malarkey and it was meant to be fun! For some maybe!

What was that noise? It sounded as if we are about to be overpowered by marauders; this was too much. Actually, it transpired that the gentle chanting that we could hear was from the fishermen, just along the beach, who were hauling in their nets. There was relief all round. At last, it was daybreak and we were still alive. Wonders will never cease.

Without any more ado we morphed into a bunch of happy campers looking forward to relaxing and enjoying ourselves before heading off in the early afternoon. Brilliant, with that our eardrums were blasted by the piercing screams from one of the kinder in our midst. We seriously thought that she was being devoured by a shark; no, she had trodden on something vicious like a stingray and the consensus of opinion was that she needed medical assistance rather fast. That put paid to my first and last ever camping trip; shush, I can't say I was sorry.

We usually retired to the Colonel's house for sundowners after our lazy Fridays and today was no exception. Actually, I think after all the excitement we all needed a rather swift stiff one.

Normally, at this time on a Friday we were relaxed and happy, which was usually the signal to strike up the band, figuratively speaking. We had in our midst a pal who had a beautiful voice and she normally took centre stage serenading us with delightful songs, particularly from Gilbert and Sullivan, and tonight was no exception. Much to my delight, one of her party pieces was 'I'm called Little Buttercup' which has remained a firm favourite to this day.

I have to tell you that I was not blessed with much of a singing voice but it would have been terrible if I hadn't reciprocated by performing my very own version of 'A Nightingale Sang in Berkeley Square', always eagerly awaited by my adoring fans!

I had attempted to sing this song – normally out of tune – here, there and everywhere so everyone always knew what was coming and, consequently, there was usually a backing group waiting in the wings, whilst the rest of the throng usually bade a hasty retreat. As they say in the movies, 'play it again, Sam'.

We would shortly be going on leave. I did wonder, though, if we were heading home or leaving home, such is the effect Dubai had had on our very being.

Thank you for tagging along with me and sitting on my shoulder, whilst I have recounted tales of joy along with numerous tales of woe, as together we have happily meandered through this desert kingdom. I am now bidding adieu to you and Dubai, with my first port of call being London, where I hope to hear that nightingale sing in Berkeley Square.

That certain night, the night we met,

There was magic abroad in the air,

There were angels dining at the Ritz,

And a nightingale sang in Berkeley Square.

About the Author

Jan Constable came late to writing but found her forte recounting her amazing and sometimes hair-raising experiences to friends and colleagues, which she decided to commit to paper.

Born and brought up near London, Jan was educated at The Lady Eleanor Holles School in West London and in her spare time enjoyed playing tennis and sailing. Her early working life included stints in both London and Paris where she worked at the British Embassy.

In 1970 at the age of 27, she found herself catapulted into Dubai as a result of her husband's job. Dubai then was an unknown desert kingdom lapped by the Persian Gulf.

Always assuming that her destiny lay somewhere in rural England, she was not exactly equipped for this extraordinary adventure. How dull her life would have been and her tales of 'The Girl Wearing Pearls' would never have seen the light of day!

Jan never returned to live in the UK permanently and now lives in Spain

Blog www.tiptoeingintothebloodyabroad.com
Email – janstable@gmail.com
Facebook – The Adventures of a Girl Wearing Pearls
Twitter – @janstable